JOB

J. Vernon McGee

THOMAS NELSON PUBLISHERS

Nashville

Published in Nashville, Tennessee, by Thomas Nelson, Inc., and distributed in Canada by Lawson Falle, Ltd., Cambridge, Ontario.

Scripture quotations are from the KING JAMES VERSION of the Bible.

Library of Congress Cataloging-in-Publication Data

McGee, J. Vernon (John Vernon), 1904–1988
   [Thru the Bible with J. Vernon McGee]
   Thru the Bible commentary series / J. Vernon McGee.
     p.   cm.
   Reprint. Originally published: Thru the Bible with J. Vernon McGee. 1975.
   Includes bibliographical references.
   ISBN 0-8407-3267-8
   1. Bible—Commentaries. I. Title.
BS491.2.M37 1991
220.7′7—dc20   90–41340
                                        CIP

Printed in the United States of America

1 2 3 4 5 6 7 — 96 95 94 93 92 91

CONTENTS

PREFACE

The radio broadcasts of the Thru the Bible Radio five-year program were transcribed, edited, and published first in single-volume paperbacks to accommodate the radio audience.

There has been a minimal amount of further editing for this publication. Therefore, these messages are not the word-for-word recording of the taped messages which went out over the air. The changes were necessary to accommodate a reading audience rather than a listening audience.

These are popular messages, prepared originally for a radio audience. They should not be considered a commentary on the entire Bible in any sense of that term. These messages are devoid of any attempt to present a theological or technical commentary on the Bible. Behind these messages is a great deal of research and study in order to interpret the Bible from a popular rather than from a scholarly (and too-often boring) viewpoint.

We have definitely and deliberately attempted "to put the cookies on the bottom shelf so that the kiddies could get them."

The fact that these messages have been translated into many languages for radio broadcasting and have been received with enthusiasm reveals the need for a simple teaching of the whole Bible for the masses of the world.

I am indebted to many people and to many sources for bringing this volume into existence. I should express my especial thanks to my secretary, Gertrude Cutler, who supervised the editorial work; to Dr. Elliott R. Cole, my associate, who handled all the detailed work with the publishers; and finally, to my wife Ruth for tenaciously encouraging me from the beginning to put my notes and messages into printed form.

Solomon wrote, ". . . of making many books there is no end; and much study is a weariness of the flesh" (Eccl. 12:12). On a sea of books that flood the marketplace, we launch this series of THRU THE BIBLE with the hope that it might draw many to the one Book, *The Bible*.

J. Vernon McGee

The Book of

JOB

INTRODUCTION

Job is a very remarkable and marvelous book. It is the first of the poetical books which also include Psalms, Proverbs, Ecclesiastes, Song of Solomon, and Lamentations. The reference "poetical books" denotes *form* rather than imaginative or capricious content. Neither does the term *poetical* mean that it is rhythmic. Hebrew poetry is achieved by repeating an idea or "parallelism." The dialogue in the Book of Job is poetry. All the conversation is in poetic form. If you have ever read Homer's *Iliad* and *Odyssey,* you know that they are examples in secular literature of this Hebrew form.

The author of Job is unknown. It has been suggested that the writer was Moses. Other suggestions have included Ezra, Solomon, Job himself, and Elihu. Elihu, mentioned in this book, is one of the miserable comforters of Job. The idea that Elihu may be the author is based on Job 32:16–17: "When I had waited, (for they spake not, but stood still, and answered no more;) I said, I will answer also my part, I also will shew mine opinion."

This is not said in the context of conversation, but the author is expressing his own thoughts in first person. Then the conversation resumes, and it is Elihu who is speaking. This indicates that Elihu may be the author of the book.

Another interesting thing about this book is that we do not know the period in which Job lived. And we do not know where he lived. I know that it says he was in the land of Uz, but we honestly don't know

where the land of Uz was located. We cannot fix it at any particular spot. It is interesting that the time and place, which are so essential to other books, are not given here.

I would suggest that Job was written during the patriarchal period. It is possible that Job knew Jacob. The fact that the Book of Job makes no reference to the Mosaic Law nor to any of the events recorded in the Book of Exodus would seem to indicate that it was written before Exodus.

Here are the arguments which lead us to place Job in the time of the patriarchs:

1. The length of Job's life span. "After this lived Job an hundred and forty years, and saw his sons, and his sons' sons, even four generations. So Job died, being old and full of days" (Job 42:16–17). We know that at the time of the patriarchs people had long life spans such as that of Job.

2. Job acted as the high priest in his family. Since there is no mention of the children of Israel or any other priesthood, evidently this took place before they came into existence.

3. Eliphaz was descended from Esau's eldest son. "These are the names of Esau's sons; Eliphaz the son of Adah the wife of Esau, Reuel the son of Bashemath the wife of Esau" (Gen. 36:10). This would make it seem that Job was a contemporary of Jacob.

This book is a great philosophical work. There are many problems that are raised and settled by this book:

1. The Book of Job raises the issue of why the righteous suffer. I really should say that it gives one of the reasons why the righteous suffer. I do not believe that this is the primary teaching of this book, although there are a great many Bible scholars who take that position.

2. Job was written to rebuke the slander of Satan against mankind.

3. Job was written to reveal Job to himself.

4. The Book of Job teaches patience. James says, ". . . Ye have heard of the patience of Job . . ." (James 5:11). Was Job patient? I'll be honest with you, it is difficult to see how this man was patient. We'll consider this when we get to the end of the book.

5. I think the primary purpose of the Book of Job is to teach repentance. If you want to disagree with this right now, just stay with us

until we get to the end of the book, and then draw your own conclusions.

You see, when men want to talk or write about repentance, they always pick a character who has had a sinful beginning. For example, they will point out Manasseh, the most ungodly king of Judah. We studied about him back in the historical books of the Old Testament, and we saw that he repented. May I say to you, that is the kind of repentance we like to think of.

There was Saul of Tarsus, the greatest enemy the Lord Jesus Christ ever had. He repented. There was St. Francis of Assisi, a dissipated nobelman of his day, and he repented. There was Jerry MacAuley, the drunken bum on skid row in New York City, and he repented.

God didn't pick a man like that in order to teach repentance. He could have! But God selected the best man who ever lived in the time of the Old Testament, possibly the best man who ever lived with the exception of Jesus Christ. God chose this man and showed that he needed to repent. When we get to the end of this book, we find the words of Job himself. "I have heard of thee by the hearing of the ear: but now mine eye seeth thee. Wherefore I abhor myself, and repent in dust and ashes" (Job 42:5-6). This ought to teach every believer today—it should teach everyone who reads this—that no matter how good we think we are, we need to see ourselves as God sees us. All our righteousness is as filthy rags. We need to repent.

This is a great philosophical work and has been acclaimed so by many. Tennyson called this book "the greatest poem, whether of ancient or modern literature." Speaking of the Book of Job, Thomas Carlyle, the Scottish philosopher said, "I call that one of the grandest ever written with pen." Martin Luther said that this book is "more magnificent and sublime than any other book of Scripture." And Dr. Moorehead said, "The Book of Job is one of the noblest poems in existence."

The prose section of the Book of Job is a gigantic, sweeping drama that encompasses earth and heaven. This does not mean it is fiction. Job is referred to as a historical character in the Scriptures (see Ezek. 14:14, 20; James 5:11), and Paul quotes from the Book of Job (1 Cor. 3:19).

Many writers have used Job as the basis for their plots, including H. G. Wells and Archibald MacLeish in his one-time Broadway hit, J. B. In his play MacLeish attempted to make an analogy between the Book of Job and modern man. Very candidly, I think he missed it, although he mentioned the human predicament today, and he knew about that. I don't think he quite knew about Job and the great purpose of that book. His play speaks of the despair and also the hope of modern man, but beyond that I think the analogy breaks down. The Book of Job reveals a man who was very conscious of God, but who would find nothing wrong with himself, one who was very egotistical about his own righteousness and maintained it in the face of those who were around him. Job felt that before God he was all right. In fact, he wanted to come into the presence of God to defend himself. When Job did that, he found that he needed to repent!

This is not a description of modern man by any means. The psychiatrists have told man today that his problem is that his mother didn't love him as she should have. In my opinion, the thing that is wrong with this generation is that mother didn't paddle as much as she should have. But we are told that mother and father have neglected the boy and the girl. Now I admit there may be some truth to that, and perhaps this is a part of the problem. However, we cannot shift the blame to others. Modern man refuses to take the blame for his deficiencies, inabilities, and sins. He tries to put the blame on somebody else. He will not accept responsibility for himself and his own actions.

Now, there is One who bore all of our sins. Until you and I recognize that *we* are sinners and need to turn to Him, my friend, we are only putting the blame on the wrong person. I think it is pretty low for any man to put the blame for his sins on his mother. That is a terrible thing, and yet that is what we find today.

Modern man is in a real predicament, and he is in great despair. He is blaming his sin on others, and he can find no place to go to find that comfort which he craves. Instead he has surrounded himself with materialism and secularism. I knew a man once who must have had twenty-five different buttons at the headboard of his bed. He could turn on lights all over the place, have a bell ring, open and close doors, and turn on outside lights—all from his bed. I have never seen any-

thing like that. That to him was a great security. Many of us do that. We each have our own "security blanket," and we snuggle up to it.

However, the problem with modern man is that he doesn't have God in his consciousness. He doesn't know that there is a Savior to whom he can go. That is different from Job. Job was very conscious of God and trusted Him. The fact is that God will put Job through the mill, as we shall see, and will finally bring him into His very presence. God stripped Job of all his securities in order to bring him to Himself.

Modern man is being put through the mill even in an affluent society. Despite all his gadgets and comforts of life, he is adrift on a piece of driftwood out in the midst of a vast ocean, and he doesn't know where he is or where he is going. That is rather frightening. Actually, it is beginning to force some folk to think that somewhere there is a Someone. We have a song today that says to "put your hand in the hand of the Man from Galilee." Well, that is getting pretty close, but it still misses the point that modern man must come to Him as a *sinner* and must accept Him as Savior. People today talk about commitment. What *is* your commitment, by the way? You can't just say, "Lord, Lord," and expect Him to be your Lord and Master. First He must be your *Savior!* He died for you. If you don't begin with Jesus Christ at the cross, you will not begin with Him anywhere.

I have spent time on this because I think it is important. Job had a consciousness of the presence of God all the way through his troubles. He was not adrift in the sense that modern man is adrift. What Job could not understand was why God permitted him to be put through the mill. Job did not recognize that he needed to repent—until God dealt with him.

OUTLINE

I. Drama (Prose), Chapters 1—2
   A. Scene I: Land of Uz. Job's Prosperity and Serenity, 1:1–5
   B. Scene II: Heaven. Satan's Slander of God and Job, 1:6–12
   C. Scene III: Back in Land of Uz. Job's Loss of Children and Wealth. 1:13–22
   D. Scene IV: Heaven, God, and Satan, 2:1–6
   E. Scene V: Land of Uz. Job's Loss of Health and Wife's Sympathy, 2:7–10

II. Dialogue (Poetry), Chapters 2:11—42:6
   A. Scene VI: Down to the Dump of the City, 2:11—37:24
      1. Job's Loss of Understanding from Friends, 2:11–13
      2. Job vs. Eliphaz, Bildad, Zophar, 3:1—32:1
      3. Job vs. Elihu, 32:2—37:24
   B. Scene VII: Jehovah vs. Job, 38:1—42:6

III. Epilogue (Prose), Chapter 42:7–17
   Scene VIII: Land of Uz. Job's Blessings Doubled.

CHAPTER 1

THEME: Drama in heaven and on earth

LAND OF UZ

There was a man in the land of Uz, whose name was Job; and that man was perfect and upright, and one that feared God, and eschewed evil [Job 1:1].

The land of Uz was somewhere in the Middle East, but beyond that there is nothing specific known about it. The historian Josephus gives us a glimmer of light on its location. In Genesis 10:23–23 Uz is listed as a son of Aram, a son of Shem. In Genesis 22:20–21 Huz (or Uz) is the firstborn of Nahor who was Abraham's brother. Josephus tells us that Uz was the founder of the ancient city of Damascus. Damascus is, in fact, the oldest continuously inhabited city in the world. So I think we can say that Job lived somewhere in the Syrian desert.

That same desert is the place where the Lord sent the apostle Paul for his "postgraduate studies." God schooled and disciplined many of His men out on that desert. My friend, your land of Uz and my land of Uz may be in different places geographically. It could be any place on this earth. That is not the important matter. The important thing is that there are certain lessons God wants us to learn in that place.

We are told Job was *perfect*. What does it mean when it says he was perfect? It means he was perfect in his relation to God in the sense that he had offered the sacrifices (as we will see in v. 5). In those days the sacrifice was a burnt offering.

Then we read that he *feared God*. He had a high and holy concept of God and, as a result, he hated evil. You can see that he is different from modern man who is without any knowledge of God.

And there were born unto him seven sons and three daughters.

> His substance also was seven thousand sheep, and three
> thousand camels, and five hundred yoke of oxen, and
> five hundred she asses, and a very great household; so
> that this man was the greatest of all the men of the east
> [Job 1:2–3].

He had a wonderful family of ten children. He was very wealthy, and
they all lived in luxury and ease. He had camels for transportation. He
must have been in the trucking business of that day. He also had she
asses for milk. That was considered a delicacy in that day. It's one delicacy that I'm willing to miss, by the way.

This man lived in the lap of luxury. The last part of verse 3 would
indicate to us that he was Howard Hughes, John D. Rockefeller, Henry
Ford, and the oil men of Texas all rolled into one.

> And his sons went and feasted in their houses, every one
> his day; and sent and called for their three sisters to eat
> and to drink with them [Job 1:4].

They were living in the lap of luxury and certainly had it easy. But
notice that in the midst of all that plenty and ease there was a fear in
the heart of Job.

> And it was so, when the days of their feasting were gone
> about, that Job sent and sanctified them, and rose up
> early in the morning, and offered burnt offerings ac-
> cording to the number of them all: for Job said, It may be
> that my sons have sinned, and cursed God in their
> hearts. Thus did Job continually [Job 1:5].

The thing that interests me is that he didn't feel that he needed an
offering. He felt that he was right with God. But he thought that maybe
these sons and daughters weren't as close to God as they should be, so
he offered sacrifices for them. He was the high priest in his own family.

Now this is the end of scene one. It is a gorgeous scene of a wealthy man with a lovely family living with an abundance of everything. But he had one fear in his heart. It is a fear that a great many folk have today about their sons and daughters. He recognized that he couldn't cope with that problem himself, so he went to God.

My friend, there are a great many parents who are distraught today because they have a son or daughter who has left home and gotten into trouble, and is maybe even on drugs. Many of these parents have never been able to go to God themselves as Job did. As a result, they carry with them problems that they cannot solve. Job knew where to go with his fears. He offered a burnt offering for his children. That burnt offering speaks of Christ. This man is a man of God.

HEAVEN

Our next scene opens in heaven, and what a scene it is. Neither Job nor any of the other people in this book knew that this took place at all. But this scene will enable us today to understand and interpret some of the things which happen to God's people. I don't say that it is the total explanation, but it is a part of it.

Now there was a day when the sons of God came to present themselves before the LORD, and Satan came also among them [Job 1:6].

Now this is the scene in heaven. The sons of God, His created intelligences, come before Him. I must confess I know very little about them. I think they are numberless, as numberless as the sand on the seashore, which means you and I cannot count them. And they are not human beings; they do not belong to our race. Yet these are God's created intelligences, and they are responsible creatures. They must come to report to God as a matter of regular routine. That is something I suppose we would expect. But there is also something here that is rather shocking. We are told that "Satan came also among them." That is a surprise.

> **And the Lord said unto Satan, Whence comest thou?
> Then Satan answered the Lord, and said, From going to
> and fro in the earth, and from walking up and down in
> it [Job 1:7].**

By the way, Satan must also make a report. That is amazing, isn't it?
Do you think he came from hell? No, he didn't. Friends, hell hasn't
been opened up yet. No one is in hell today. It will not be opened up
until the Millennium takes place on this earth. Hell is the place prepared for the Devil and his angels, but they are not there yet. The fact
of the matter is that Satan has as much access to this earth as you and I
have, and more so.

This earth is the domain of Satan. He has not been in hell. He says
that he has been going up and down—east, west, north, and south—
on this earth. Remember that Scripture calls him ". . . the god of this
world . . ." (2 Cor. 4:4) and ". . . the prince of the power of the air . . ."
(Eph. 2:2). So that we know that he has great access and freedom on
this earth today. We are warned by Peter, "Be sober, be vigilant; because your adversary the devil, as a roaring lion, walketh about, seek-
ing whom he may devour" (1 Peter 5:8). My friend, this is a warning,
and this is exactly what we are told here in the Book of Job. Satan
himself said that he has the freedom to go up and down this earth.

You remember that when Satan tempted the Lord Jesus he offered to
Him the kingdoms of this earth. The Lord Jesus never said, "You don't
have them to offer." He simply refused the temptation. Apparently
those kingdoms are accessible to Satan, and he has that kind of freedom.

When you look at this earth today, it does look like Satan is running
things, does it not? God is overruling all things, but He has given Satan
a period of freedom. We are told that this world in which you and I live
is controlled by Satan. He must be overcome, and we can only overcome him by the blood of the Lamb. Now this is quite a revelation,
isn't it? And it is contrary to modern thinking.

> **And the Lord said unto Satan, Hast thou considered my
> servant Job, that there is none like him in the earth, a**

perfect and an upright man, one that feareth God, and escheweth evil? [Job 1:8].

God gives a good report of Job. He says he is an outstanding man. It would seem that Satan has been trying to get at Job. I draw that conclusion from Satan's next statement.

Then Satan answered the LORD, and said, Doth Job fear God for nought?

Hast not thou made an hedge about him, and about his house, and about all that he hath on every side? thou hast blessed the work of his hands, and his substance is increased in the land [Job 1:9–10].

Apparently Satan had been trying to get through to Job and made the discovery that he couldn't get through to him because there was a hedge about him. He tells the Lord, "You have put a hedge around him, and I can't touch him."

I believe that there is a hedge about every believer today, and I do not think that Satan can touch you unless God permits it. And if God permits it, it will be for His purpose. That is what this book teaches us.

But put forth thine hand now, and touch all that he hath, and he will curse thee to thy face [Job 1:11].

Now Satan casts this slur upon Job. I think he despises mankind. He suggests that Job is really a timeserver to God. And Satan has no use for you or me. He says we are timeservants and that if God took down that hedge and took everything from us, we would curse God.

Mind you, there are a lot of people in the world who would curse God. There is no question about that. All one needs to do is listen to men on the street here in Southern California. I hear God cursed nearly every day.

One day I walked by a construction site where one of the foremen was attempting to make some sort of an adjustment. It didn't work and

the piece fell down. My, he began to curse God. Now he may go to church on Sunday and carry a big Bible under his arm—I don't know about that. But I do know this, he cursed God. We hear that constantly today. Men are not rightly related to God, my friend.

This man Job had a hedge around him, and when Satan found he couldn't touch him, he said, "I'd like to get to him." Satan hates mankind. Why in the world anyone wants to serve Satan is more than I know, because he despises us. I wouldn't want a master like that. I want a master who will love me and be sympathetic toward me. And that is the kind of Master I have.

> **And the Lord said unto Satan, Behold, all that he hath is in thy power; only upon himself put not forth thine hand. So Satan went forth from the presence of the Lord [Job 1:12].**

We learn here that sometimes God permits Satan to take away from us those things that we lean on. I know that when our little security blanket is taken away from us we feel so helpless, incapable, and lost in this world. Many of us cry out to God at such a time.

Notice that God is going to permit Satan to take all Job's possessions from him. Believe me, Satan would destroy us if he could. He has slandered both God and Job, implying that God is not worthy to be served and loved for Himself alone, but that He must pay Job to love Him. Satan is the enemy of God and man.

BACK IN THE LAND OF UZ

> **And there was a day when his sons and his daughters were eating and drinking wine in their eldest brother's house [Job 1:13].**

Job's children were having a high old time, friends. They were going around from one brother's house to another, and it was a banquet every day. They were really living it up.

And there came a messenger unto Job, and said, The oxen were plowing, and the asses feeding beside them:

And the Sabeans fell upon them, and took them away; yea, they have slain the servants with the edge of the sword; and I only am escaped alone to tell thee [Job 1:14–15].

Here Job has been having a rather nice life, and then suddenly things begin to happen. He didn't even know he had enemies like this, but now the Sabeans come in and take away his cattle.

While he was yet speaking, there came also another, and said, The fire of God is fallen from heaven, and hath burned up the sheep, and the servants, and consumed them; and I only am escaped alone to tell thee [Job 1:16].

"The fire of God." That is interesting. I kid a friend of mine who is an insurance agent. You know the policy always states they are not liable if your house is destroyed by "an act of God." We always blame God if something is destroyed. They were saying the same thing in that day. Why didn't he say, "The fire of Satan"? Who did it? Why, Satan did it! Why don't the insurance policies say, "If God permits Satan to destroy my house"?

While he was yet speaking, there came also another, and said, The Chaldeans made out three bands, and fell upon the camels, and have carried them away, yea, and slain the servants with the edge of the sword; and I only am escaped alone to tell thee [Job 1:17].

We talk about the crash of the stock market. I tell you, Job had real stock, and it was all taken away. Everything was wiped out.

While he was yet speaking, there came also another, and said, Thy sons and thy daughters were eating and drinking wine in their eldest brother's house:

> **And, behold, there came a great wind from the wilderness, and smote the four corners of the house, and it fell upon the young men, and they are dead; and I only am escaped alone to tell thee [Job 1:18–19].**

Here is a tragedy beyond tragedies. All of his children are slain. A real Texas-style tornado hit that house and all his children were killed. What would you do in a case like that? Notice what Job does:

> **Then Job arose, and rent this mantle, and shaved his head, and fell down upon the ground, and worshipped,**
>
> **And said, Naked came I out of my mother's womb, and naked shall I return thither: the LORD gave, and the LORD hath taken away; blessed be the name of the LORD.**
>
> **In all this Job sinned not, nor charged God foolishly [Job 1:20–22].**

Watch this man and listen to his testimony. Here is a viewpoint of life and a philosophy of life that Christians need today toward material things. You and I came into this world with nothing. We were naked as jaybirds when we came into this world. And we are going to leave the world the same way. Remember the old bromide, "There are no pockets in a shroud"? My friend, you can't take anything with you.

The story is told that years ago all the relatives were standing outside the bedroom door of the patriarch of a very wealthy family. They were waiting for the old man to die and for the family lawyer to come out. When he came, he announced to them all that the father had died. Immediately one of the more greedy ones asked, "How much did he leave?" And the lawyer replied, "He left it all. He didn't take anything with him."

That is the way it will be with all of us. It makes no difference how many deeds you have or how strong your safety deposit box may be, what you accumulate or how much insurance you have. When you go and when I go, we're going just like we came into this world. It is very important for us to get this into our philosophy of life. You may be

living today in an expensive home, or you may be living in a hovel. You may have a big bank account, or you may not have anything to count at all. You may have a safety deposit box filled with stocks and bonds, or you may not even have a safety deposit box. It makes no difference who you are. We're all going to leave the same way we came into this world. Whatever you have, you are simply a steward of it. Really, in the final analysis, it does not belong to you, does it?

This man Job falls down, and he worships God. Oh yes, he rent his mantle, he shaved his head, and you could have heard this man weeping half a mile away. He has lost everything, even his sons and his daughters. But he says, "The LORD gave, and the LORD hath taken away; blessed be the name of the LORD."

My friend, whatever you have, the Lord gave it to you. And He can take it away if He wishes. He is going to hold you and me responsible for how we use the things He permits us to have. That is the reason that in 2 Corinthians Paul calls us all "stewards." A steward handles what belongs to someone else. God is going to ask us how we used His material things. Everything down here is His, and you are just using them. When you leave, you won't be taking them with you.

Job understood this, and he did not lose his faith. He is still holding on to God. "In all this Job sinned not, nor charged God foolishly."

CHAPTER 2

THEME: *Heaven, God, and Satan; land of Uz; down to the dump of the city*

HEAVEN, GOD, AND SATAN

Again there was a day when the sons of God came to present themselves before the LORD and Satan came also among them to present himself before the LORD [Job 2:1].

The created intelligences make their regular report again. Notice that they all had to report to God. You and I are going to have to report to God some day. Remember that the Christian is going to stand at the judgment seat of Christ (2 Cor. 5:10), and there we are going to report on our stewardship on earth. We are going to give an account to Him. (As believers we will not stand at the Great White Throne Judgment of Revelation 20:11–15), which is where the unbeliever must give his account.) All the creatures of God must come to make their report to Him.

Remember, my friend, He is God. We are not operating freely today. We hear the cry all around us, "We want liberty." How much liberty do we have? A grasshopper can jump higher than a man can jump, size for size. If we could jump like a grasshopper, we could jump over the tallest building. God created us with certain limitations. We are creatures. He is the Creator. We must all answer to Him.

When these sons of God came to present themselves to Him, notice that Satan also had to come to give his report. He is not beyond the jurisdiction of God. Although God already knew what he would report, Satan had to appear before God and tell the Lord what he had been doing.

And the LORD said unto Satan, From whence comest thou? And Satan answered the LORD, and said, From go-

**ing to and fro in the earth, and from walking up and
down in it [Job 2:2].**

In other words, Satan again reports that he has been down in his baili-
wick. He was running this place down here. I believe he still runs it,
friend. Just look around you and see who runs this world.

> **And the LORD said unto Satan, Hast thou considered my
> servant Job, that there is none like him in the earth, a
> perfect and an upright man, one that feareth God, and
> escheweth evil? and still he holdeth fast his integrity, al-
> though thou movedst me against him, to destroy him
> without cause [Job 2:3].**

Now this shows us clearly that what the Lord allowed Satan to do with
Job was done without a cause in Job. People are always saying, "Why
does God let this happen to me?" Perhaps the answer from the Lord is,
"There is no reason for it in you. I am not spanking you. I am not
punishing you. I just want to bring you closer to Me." That is what He
did with Job. It was without a cause in Job.

Sometimes we point our finger at some believer and say that God is
whipping him, which may not be true at all. It may be that God is
testing him in a way He cannot test you or me, because He couldn't
trust us with that much trouble. Very frankly, I would never want to go
through what Job had to suffer!

The Lord calls Satan's attention to Job again. "Job is still serving
Me. You said that if I would permit you to take everything away from
Job, he would turn his back on Me—but he hasn't done that. He has
maintained his integrity."

> **And Satan answered the LORD, and said, Skin for skin,
> yea, all that a man hath will he give for his life.**
>
> **But put forth thine hand now, and touch his bone and
> his flesh, and he will curse thee to thy face.**

And the LORD said unto Satan, Behold, he is in thine hand; but save his life [Job 2:4–6].

You know, Satan is accurate about most of us. There is a chink in our armor. We have our Achilles' heel—that certain weakness. When we get right down to the bare bones, we all cave in. But God has given us a promise: "There hath no temptation taken you but such as is common to man: but God is faithful, who will not suffer you to be tempted above that ye are able; but will with the temptation also make a way to escape, that ye may be able to bear it" (1 Cor. 10:13). God will never allow us to be tempted beyond what we can stand. We need to recognize that.

My friend, wherever you are and whatever you are going through, God is able to sustain you. That is a great comfort. We do not know what a day may bring forth. It could be tragic beyond words or it could be a delightful, wonderful day. Whichever it is, God says, "I will enable you to get through it." God will see to it that our armor stands up. That is a wonderful thing to know.

Satan is a liar. Satan says that Job will give anything for his own body and that if he is allowed to touch Job's bone and flesh, Job will curse God.

LAND OF UZ

So went Satan forth from the presence of the LORD, and smote Job with sore boils from the sole of his foot unto his crown.

And he took him a potsherd to scrape himself withal; and he sat down among the ashes [Job 2:7–8].

This man is being tested in every part of his life. Satan is attempting to break him down, of course. He has lost his finances, he has lost his family, and now his physical body is being attacked.

There is seemingly no human explanation for the troubles of Job. It is not a punishment for his sins, and the whole thing would be senseless without proper insight. That is the reason God gives the explana-

tion to us at the beginning of the book so *we* will be able to understand. What was happening to Job was for a lofty and worthy purpose. There was a good and sufficient reason in the internal counsels of God. When all the facts were in and all the facets considered, God had a purpose in it. It was discipline. We can say that it was good for Job.

When father whips little Willy, he says, "This hurts me more than it hurts you." Little Willy answers, "Yes, but not in the same place." This experience was for Job's ultimate good. Remember that God's ways are not our ways, "For as the heavens are higher than the earth, so are my ways higher than your ways, and my thoughts than your thoughts" (Isa. 55:9).

We try to deliver our children from suffering; we do all we can to prevent it. We give them everything we can afford to make life pleasant for them, and we spoil them. We have raised a spoiled generation.

A day came when Job realized that something good was coming out of his experience, but at first he did not understand at all. Not only was it for the good of Job, but it was for the glory of God. Remember that God's character had been impugned by Satan. I think all the created intelligences in heaven shuddered when they heard Satan cast that aspersion on God. His implication was: You're not worthy to be loved. You have to *pay* Job to love You and serve You. You have paid lovers.

How about it, friend? Are we just timeservers? Are we paid lovers? God is good and God is merciful to us. We rejoice in His goodness. But it is when we are under trial that we reveal our true metal. The fires always burn out the dross, you know, and testing reveals that which is genuine. We are to be lights in this world. Light is for the darkness, and God puts us in the darkness so that our lights will shine.

God has not promised an easy life to any of His children. On the contrary, we are told that the way will be rough. If we suffer with Him we will reign with Him. If there is no pain, there will be no pomp. If there is no suffering, no struggle, then there will be no sceptre either. It is difficult for us to bow under the awful hand of Almighty God. This is why Paul wrote, "Knowing therefore the terror of the Lord, we persuade men . . ." (2 Cor. 5:11).

What kind of trouble did Job have? We are told that he had sore boils and that he scraped himself with a potsherd, that is, a piece of broken pottery. There has been a great deal of speculation among Christian doctors about what Job's illness might have been. Dr. Cedric Harvey was an English doctor in London who suggested that Job was actually a victim of psychosomatic dermatitis. Now there is a good one for you. The Word of God says he was covered with boils, and this Christian doctor says he had psychosomatic dermatitis. That shows what becoming a doctor can do for you.

Psychosomatic dermatitis is a disease of the skin induced by anxiety. Well, I don't think that is the explanation of it, but the doctor couldn't be there to diagnose it personally anyway, so I can contradict him. Dr. Harvey has written about this in a medical magazine. He goes on to say that a study of the book points up Job's insomnia, terrifying dreams, general state of anxiety, all now generally accepted as symptoms of psychosomatic dermatitis. Remember this the next time you have to scratch yourself. At least you will know the name of your disease.

Dr. Charles J. Brim, a New York heart specialist, diagnosed Job's illness as pellagra, a vitamin deficiency disease. Now you can take your choice between these two diagnoses. As a matter of fact, it has even been suggested that he had cancer. I hope you won't mind if I just say he had boils. Whatever it was, this man was in real trouble.

Satan moved in on Job to take away from him all that any man rests upon in dignity in this life. Now we are introduced to his wife. Listen to her!

> **Then said his wife unto him, Dost thou still retain thine integrity? curse God, and die [Job 2:9].**

Satan wants to get him so beaten down that he doesn't even want to call himself a man.

His wife's suggestion to curse God and die is strange advice coming from a wife. Apparently she wanted to be a widow. However, it might be a tender suggestion, because she could see the suffering that

he was going through. Satan removed everything else that Job had. Why didn't he remove his wife, too? I think the reason is that his wife wasn't any help to Job. It would seem that she actually would do the devil's bidding.

> **But he said unto her, Thou speakest as one of the foolish women speaketh. What? shall we receive good at the hand of God, and shall we not receive evil? In all this did not Job sin with his lips [Job 2:10].**

Job did maintain his integrity.

This is now the actual beginning of the book. We have shown how Job has been attacked and how he has maintained his integrity. Now the friends of Job come to visit and "comfort" him. Now his integrity will really be attacked. This is where the dialogue begins.

DOWN TO THE DUMP OF THE CITY

> **Now when Job's three friends heard of all this evil that was come upon him, they came every one from his own place; Eliphaz the Temanite, and Bildad the Shuhite, and Zophar the Naamathite: for they had made an appointment together to come to mourn with him and to comfort him [Job 2:11].**

Now we are introduced to the three friends, and we need to get to know them. Eliphaz was a Temanite. Teman was a grandson of Esau according to Genesis 36:10–11. Bildad was a Shuhite. Shuah was a son of Abraham according to Genesis 25:2. Zophar was a Naamathite. Naamah was in northern Arabia. These facts lead us to place the time of Job at the time of the patriarchs and also give us the general location where Job lives, although we do not know the specific spot.

These men came to mourn with Job. Since I am going to say some very ugly things about his friends, I think I ought to say what I can that is good about them. They were real friends to Job until this happened

to him. This experience alienated them from Job, and the reason it did was that they did not know God nor did they know why God does certain things.

This is a good reason why even today many of us should be very careful about trying to explain why certain things happen to other people. We have no right to say that God has let something happen to So-and-so for such-and-such a reason. We may think it is a good reason, but the problem is that we really don't *know* the reason.

These friends of Job were just as sure of their reasons as people are today. They thought they knew why certain things happened, but they were entirely wrong.

However, note that they were real friends to Job.

> **And when they lifted up their eyes afar off, and knew him not, they lifted up their voices, and wept: and they rent every one his mantle, and sprinkled dust upon their heads toward heaven.**
>
> **So they sat down with him upon the ground seven days and seven nights, and none spake a word unto him: for they saw that his grief was very great [Job 2:12–13].**

They had heard that their friend Job was in trouble, but they didn't dream it was as severe as it really was. The last time they had seen Job he was in a beautiful home with his fine sons and daughters around him. They had seen the wealth of Job spread there upon the landscape. Now they had come to visit him. They probably at least expected to find him in his luxurious home, but here they find him out at the dump heap of the town where they emptied the garbage, and he is scraping himself with an old broken piece of pottery. He doesn't have anything at all. *Everything* is gone. Poor Job.

These friends mourned and wept and howled. For seven days they just sat there and didn't say a word. They sat with Job for seven days and seven nights! I would say they were friends. As far as they knew how, they tried to comfort him by just sitting there with him for seven days. Although they mourned for him during this full time, they were

in no position to comfort him for three reasons: (1) They did not understand God; (2) they did not understand Job; and (3) they did not understand themselves.

As they sit for seven days of mourning, Job is under their critical gaze, and they shake their heads in a knowing manner. They are all brilliant men. They are all philosophers, men who do a great deal of thinking, and they all come to one conclusion. They come to it from different angles, but the conclusion is the same: *Job must be an awful sinner for these things to happen to him. God must be punishing him. He had better get his life straightened out.* This is the conclusion of each of them.

Finally Job just can't stand it any longer. They are beginning to shake their heads in a knowing way with a smirk on their faces. They seem to say, "Aha, brother Job, it finally comes out. You've been living in sin, and you gave the impression that you were such a pious individual. Now we know that this has come to you because your sin is out at last." Well, Job just can't take that. He can take everything else that has happened to him, but not a false accusation. So the dialogue begins. Job is the first to speak. Listen to the heartbreak of this man in the chapter that follows.

CHAPTER 3

THEME: Job's first discourse—his complaint

We have seen that Job is being made a test case; he is a guinea pig. Satan has challenged God. He has said to God, "You have put a hedge around Job and have given him everything. But if those things are taken away from him, he will curse You to Your face!" Satan was casting a slur upon mankind and a blasphemy upon God. The intelligences of heaven must have cringed and certainly blushed when they heard this highest creature, whom God had created and who had fallen, cast such a slur upon the Almighty God.

God permitted Satan to get at this man Job. Satan began to move into this man's life. We have seen how he took one thing after another away from him in order to break him down. Before we go into the dialogues, I think we ought to pause and see the background of all this again.

You and I belong to a lost race. It is difficult to think that you and I are living down here among a bunch of liars and cut-throats and thieves and murderers. We say, "But *I'm* not like that." I'm afraid you are—all of us are. We belong to that kind of race. That is the reason God cannot take us to heaven as we are. After all, if God took the world to heaven as it is today, we wouldn't have anything but just the world all over again. I don't know how you feel about it, but I see no reason just to duplicate this all again. And God apparently sees no reason to do it either. Therefore He is not taking us to heaven as we are. That is the reason the Lord Jesus had to say to a refined, polished, religious Pharisee, ". . . Ye must be *born* again" (John 3:7). If it is any comfort to any of us, we are all in the same boat. We talk about "normal" behavior today. A psychologist is great at that. How in the world does he arrive at a definition of "normal" behavior? What he does is to plot a chart, and where the majority of people are, that is what he calls normal. At one end are the abnormal and at the other end are the supernormal—there are a few who fall at either end of the chart. How does he know

that the mass of people in the middle are normal? I don't think they are. God says we are *all* in sin.

This creature called man is frail, feeble, and faulty. It is easy to upset the equilibrium of any man. It can happen to any of us. It is easy to depart from the pattern and to tip the scale. Statistics reveal that one out of ten people spends time in a mental institution, and the number keeps increasing.

God has placed certain props about man to make man stand straight and upright. The Book of Ecclesiastes puts it like this: "Lo, this only have I found, that God hath made man upright; but they have sought out many inventions" (Eccl. 7:29). God has clothed man with an armor of protection, a security, if you please. God has given certain aids to all men, godly and ungodly alike. He makes it rain on the just and on the unjust. The wicked get just as much sunshine and air to breathe, and their heart is just as good as those who are the godly, the believers in Christ. The Devil knows that if he can get to a man, remove the props, strip him of every vestige of aid, take away his security blanket, he can upset him and turn him upside down, destroy his morale, rearrange his thinking, brainwash him. Therefore, God has placed a hedge about man to keep the Devil away. Sometimes Satan is permitted to crash the gate, and he will strip a man down to his naked soul. God permitted the Devil to brainwash Job.

The Book of Job presents the problem. It describes the stripping of a man's soul. It does not give the solution, although answers are suggested. You must go to the New Testament for the real answer. It is sort of like the algebra book I had at school. The problems were in the front of the book and the answers were in the back. The Bible is like that. You get the problem here, but you must turn over to the New Testament to get the answer.

In many respects the Old Testament is a very unsatisfactory book. Nothing is actually solved in it. As someone has put it: The Old Testament is *expectation*; the New Testament is *realization*.

In chapters 1 and 2, the Devil has been brainwashing Job. He has stripped Job of every vestige of covering. We need to look at this because it will help us as we enter this dialogue that Job has with his friends.

1. Satan stripped Job of material substance. One of the basic needs of man is material substance. An animal is already born with a coat on. When you and I came into the world, someone had to furnish us with a coat. Later on, we had to buy our own coat. We have to have food and clothing and shelter. Man needs flocks, herds, barns, and lands. He needs to have things about him. He needs a home. Scripture tells us that God has given us all things richly to enjoy. God wants man to enjoy the things that He has put in this world. Although the curse of sin is on this world, God has provided for man in a very wonderful way.

Physical things can be spiritual blessings. Prosperity is a gift of God. There is nothing wrong in building bigger bars. The danger lies in *depending* on these things, leaning upon them as if that is all there is to life.

Actually, I think the prosperity and the affluence of the United States has been giving us a bad conscience for a long time. We have spent billions of dollars passing out crumbs to other countries in order that we might enjoy what we have. It has been to no avail because all we are doing is salving a bad conscience. Our gadgets and our conveniences and our comforts have created almost a prison for us. On holiday weekends I am amazed to see droves of people fleeing to the desert or to the seashore to get away from their electric blankets, their TV sets, their push-button kitchens. They want to rough it, they say. They feel as if they are in prison. The Christian today needs to get alone and take an inventory of himself: "Am I trusting in *things* or am I trusting in God?"

Job lost all. He went from prosperity to poverty. Job was moved, but he wasn't removed from the foundation.

2. God permitted Satan to take away Job's loved ones. You and I need loved ones to prop us up. I think the reason the Lord makes little babies so attractive is so that we will cuddle them and hug them. That is what they need. The biggest thrill I ever had in my life was to hold in my arms our first child, and the Lord took that child. The greatest thrill I have today is to hold our little grandsons. How wonderful it is. God has made us that way.

When the child grows older, he still goes to parents for love and

sympathy. He hurts his little finger and runs to mama to kiss it. You know that doesn't do it a bit of good, but it sure helps him. Without this kind of love the child develops conflicts and complexes. I believe the psychologist is right about that.

Then the time comes for the little eaglet to be pushed out of the nest. The teenager becomes less dependent on the parent, and then one day the love is transferred to someone else. Finally the love passes on to his own children. But we always need loved ones.

Poor old Job lost all of his children in one day—seven sons and three daughters!

3. Health is a great factor in the well-being of man. I notice that when the paper lists suicides it often says, "So-and-so had been in ill health." There are countless numbers of saints who have been bed-ridden and laid aside from normal activity by ill health. Perhaps they have learned to trust God in a way that you and I have not. Satan was permitted to take away Job's health. That was a tremendous blow to him.

4. Then Job lost the love and sympathy of a companion. God gave Adam a helpmeet. A "helpmeet" means the "other half" of him, the responder, the other part of him. I think God has a rib for every man; that is, He has a wife for him. God has instituted marriage for the welfare and happiness of man. Many a man who stands at the forge of life today, faithful and strong, facing the battle and daily grind, goes home and pillows his head on the breast or in the lap of a wife who understands him, and maybe he even sobs out his soul to her. How wonderful that is! Job had lost the sympathy and compassion of his wife, as we have seen.

5. Job's friends came to mourn with him, but he found that they were just a mirage on the desert. When he saw them coming, he thought they were an oasis, but they were only a mirage, and he finally calls them "miserable comforters." We are going to see why.

Now what else can the devil do to Job? He has removed all his props. Now Satan will move in and destroy Job's whole set of values. This is the thing we need to watch as we study the dialogues that ensue.

6. Job loses his sense of worth and the dignity of his own personal-

ity. What shall a man give in exchange for his soul? God pity the young people today who throw away their lives for a pill or to please a group of evil-minded companions. *It is God who attaches real value to man.* The Lord Jesus said, ". . . Ye are of more value than many sparrows" (Luke 12:7). Yet He tells us that that the Father knows all the sparrows and when they fall. Do you know what proves we are of more value? It is that Christ died for us. That tells us how much we are worth. We are worth the blood of Jesus Christ!

It was during the Dark Ages that Mueritus, a brilliant scholar, fell sick and was picked up on the highway. The doctors, thinking he was a bum, began talking about him in Latin. They said, "Shall we operate on this worthless creature?" Mueritus understood Latin very well. He raised up and answered them in Latin, "Do not call a creature worthless for whom Christ died." Remember that the Devil tries to cause us to lose our sense of worth and the dignity of our own personality.

7. Job will lose his sense of the justice of God, and he will become critical and cynical before it is over. In studying this book we need to realize that it is inspired just as all of the Bible is inspired, but not all that the characters say is true. This is an illustration of what I mean: the Devil was not inspired to tell a lie to Eve when he said, ". . . Ye shall not surely die" (Gen. 3:4), but the record of his lying is inspired. Some folk believe that every statement they find in the Bible is true, but we need to notice carefully who is making the statement. In the Book of Job we will find these men saying things that are not true.

8. Job will lose his sense of the love of God. The man who said, ". . . the LORD gave , and the LORD hath taken away; blessed be the name of the LORD" (Job 1:21), is the same man who later cried, "For the arrows of the Almighty are within me, the poison whereof drinketh up my spirit: the terrors of God do set themselves in array against me" (Job 6:4). Then in chapter 9 we hear his cry as, "Oh, that there were a daysman to stand between us." In other words, "Oh, that there were someone to take hold of the hand of God and take hold of my hand and bring us together!" We will need to go to the New Testament to find the answer to this cry of Job: "For there is one God, and one mediator between God and men, the man Christ Jesus" (1 Tim. 2:5). Thank God you and I have Someone who is our daysman!

I have spent time on this because it is very important to get this background in order to understand the dialogue which begins here and continues through chapter 37.

There are three rounds of speeches: (1) By Job, then Eliphaz, and Job answers him, (2) by Bildad, and Job answers him, and (3) by Zophar, and Job answers him. This is repeated three times with one exception—Zophar does not give a third speech. The dialogue is in the nature of a contest.

Job's friends have been sitting with him for seven days. Finally Job explodes, under the critical and accusing eyes of his friends, with his tale of woe and a wish that he had never been born.

JOB'S FIRST DISCOURSE

After this opened Job his mouth, and cursed his day.

And Job spake, and said,

Let the day perish wherein I was born, and the night in which it was said, There is a man child conceived.

Let that day be darkness; let not God regard it from above, neither let the light shine upon it.

Let darkness and the shadow of death stain it; let a cloud dwell upon it; let the blackness of the day terrify it [Job 3:1–5].

This is a very beautiful speech, very flowery, but when you add it all up, boil it down, and strain it, he is simply saying, "I wish I hadn't been born." How many times have you said that? I'm of the opinion that many of us have said it, especially when we were young and something disappointed us. This is what Job is saying, only he is saying it in poetic language.

As for that night, let darkness seize upon it; let it not be joined unto the days of the year, let it not come into the number of the months.

Lo, let that night be solitary, let no joyful voice come therein.

Let them curse it that curse the day, who are ready to raise up their mourning.

Let the stars of the twilight thereof be dark; let it look for light, but have none; neither let it see the dawning of the day:

Because it shut not up the doors of my mother's womb, nor hid sorrow from mine eyes.

Why died I not from the womb? why did I not give up the ghost when I came out of the belly?

Why did the knees prevent me? or why the breasts that I should suck? [Job 3:6–12].

Job is saying loud and clear, "I wish I had never been born." It is interesting, my friend, that this attitude never solves any problems of this
life. You may wish you had never been born, but you can't undo the
fact that you have been born. You may wish that you could die, but you
will not die by wishing. It is all a waste of time. It may help a person let
off some steam. That seems to be what it does for Job now.

> **For now should I have lain still and been quiet, I should
> have slept: then had I been at rest,**

> **With kings and counsellors of the earth, which built
> desolate places for themselves [Job 3:13–14].**

They built great monuments or great pyramids for themselves.

> **Or with princes that had gold, who filled their houses
> with silver:**

> **Or as an hidden untimely birth I had not been; as in-
> fants which never saw light [Job 3:15–16].**

He wishes he had been stillborn. Job complains that this oblivion has
been denied him. He describes death as the great equalizer. All sleep
equally.

There are two things Job is saying in this chapter. He wishes that he
had never been born. However, having been born, he wishes that he
had died at birth. These are his two wishes in this chapter, and he
finds no relief from his misery.

> **There the wicked cease from troubling; and there the
> weary be at rest.**

> **There the prisoners rest together; they hear not the voice
> of the oppressor.**

> **The small and great are there; and the servant is free
> from his master.**

Wherefore is light given to him that is in misery, and life unto the bitter in soul;

Which long for death, but it cometh not; and dig for it more than for hid treasures;

Which rejoice exceedingly, and are glad, when they can find the grave?

Why is light given to a man whose way is hid, and whom God hath hedged in?

For my sighing cometh before I eat, and my roarings are poured out like the waters [Job 3:17-24].

He pictures death as being preferred to life. He says that life is such a burden. He doesn't want to live. He would rather die. Job says he would welcome death like a miner who is digging for gold and gives a shout of joy when he finds it. He is in a desperate, desolate condition.

For the thing which I greatly feared is come upon me, and that which I was afraid of is come unto me.

I was not in safety, neither had I rest, neither was I quiet; yet trouble came [Job 3:25-26].

Job had been dwelling in peace and prosperity in the land of Uz, and things had been going so well with him. He was living in the lap of luxury. Everyone was saying, "Look at Job. He certainly has a wonderful life." Job says, "At that very moment, I was living in fear. And the thing that I dreaded has come upon me." His tranquility even in his days of prosperity was disturbed by the uncertainty of life.

I think that is a fear of a great many people today. They fear that something terrible is going to happen to them. Our problem is that we grab for our security blanket instead of grabbing for the Savior. We ought to be using our Bible for our blanket instead of turning to other things. We need to *rest* upon the Word of God.

One would almost get the impression that Job has lost his faith. He

actually has not. This is the bitter complaint of a man who is tasting the very dregs in the bottom of the cup of life. Trouble has come upon him and he does not understand at all why it should have come.

It is a monologue of complaint as friends sit around him. The language is tremendous, but Job does not have the answer. It is black pessimism.

CHAPTERS 4 AND 5

THEME: The first discourse of Eliphaz, the voice of experience

Job's three friends had been sitting with him for seven days, and they have been wagging their heads as if to say, "Mmm, it finally caught up with you!" It seems that Job could take all his suffering, but he couldn't take this attitude from his friends. He broke out in a monologue of complaint and whining. It is black pessimism and has no answer to the problem at all.

Now his three friends will begin to talk to him. The first will be Eliphaz and then Bildad and finally Zophar. The names of these men actually give us just a little pen picture of them.

Eliphaz means "God is strength" or "God is fine gold."

Bildad means "son of contention." He is a mean one, by the way. He is actually brutal and blunt and crude in his method.

Zophar means "a sparrow." He twitters. He has a mean tongue and makes terrible insinuations to Job.

The dialogue that takes place is a real contest. These friends are actually going to make an attack on Job, and he will respond. This is what we might call intellectual athletics. This type of thing was popular in that day. Today people go to a football game or a baseball, basketball, or hockey game—something athletic where the physical is demonstrated. In those days people gathered for intellectual contests. I think that by the time this dialogue was under way a great crowd had gathered, listening to what was taking place.

We want to think that those people were not civilized; yet they put the emphasis on the intellectual. And we consider ourselves to be such civilized people who have advanced so far, but we put the emphasis on the physical. We are not as superior to these ancient people as we would like to think.

Job has just broken out with a complaint. He is in the deepest, blackest pessimism that a man can be in. The Devil has stripped him

of everything. He has nothing left to lean on, no place to turn. Even God seems very far removed from him at this particular time.

Eliphaz is the first to speak. He is the voice of experience. He is a remarkable man, and he relates a strange and mysterious experience. The key to what he has to say is found in verse 8, "Even as I have seen." Everything he has to say rests on that. He is the voice of experience. He has had a remarkable vision and has heard secrets that nobody else has ever heard.

> **Then Eliphaz the Temanite answered and said,**
>
> **If we assay to commune with thee, wilt thou be grieved? but who can withhold himself from speaking [Job 4:1–2].**

He begins in a diplomatic sort of way, but one gets the feeling he has his tongue in his cheek. This is a sort of false politeness. He says to Job, "Do you mind if I say something?" Then he adds, "Regardless of whether or not you mind my saying something, I'm going to say it." And he does.

> **Behold, thou hast instructed many, and thou hast strengthened the weak hands.**
>
> **Thy words have upholden him that was falling, and thou hast strengthened the feeble knees.**
>
> **But now it is come upon thee, and thou faintest; it toucheth thee, and thou art troubled [Job 4:3–5].**

He is saying to Job, "In the old days when you were in prosperity and plenty and in good health, you were a tower of strength to everybody else. You could advise them. You could speak to them and tell them what to do. You knew how to help those who were in trouble. But now something has happened to you, and you have folded up. You're just a paper doll; you're just a paper tiger. You were never real at all. The advice you gave to others—can't you follow it yourself?"

I would say that that is the problem a great many of us have today. Isn't it interesting that we can always tell the other person what he should do when troubles come to him? It is like the cartoon of two psychiatrists meeting one day. One looked at the other and said, "You are fine. How am I?" We are always analyzing the other fellow, telling him how *he* is.

Eliphaz accuses Job of being an expert at that. In a very sarcastic manner he says, "Now it has happened to you, and what have you done? You folded up."

> **Is not this thy fear, thy confidence, thy hope, and the uprightness of thy ways? [Job 4:6].**

"Isn't your own advice good enough for you? It helped others; now it ought to help you."

Now Eliphaz makes an insinuation to Job. But he does it in a polite way. We will find that Job's other two friends are more blunt and crude, especially old Zophar.

> **Remember, I pray thee, who ever perished, being innocent? or where were the righteous cut off? [Job 4:7].**

He accuses Job of having a chink in his armor, of having an Achilles' heel. He says this would not have happened to Job if there hadn't been something radically wrong in his life, something that he is keeping secret. This is the argument. He is making an insinuation, and it's not true of Job. I hear this verse quoted even today, and it's not interpreted accurately, my friend.

Now we know this insinuation is wrong and is not true of Job, because at the beginning of the book God gave us that scene in heaven so that we might know Job and understand his character. These friends will be miserable comforters because they do not understand God, they do not understand Job, and they do not understand themselves.

There are too many people who try to deal with spiritual matters who are not qualified to do so. Very candidly, that is one of the reasons I am reluctant to counsel folk. My feeling is that if a person is a child of

God—unless it is a technical matter, a theological matter, or some physical difficulty—it can be settled between the soul and God. We don't need to go to the third person. After all, we have an Intercessor with God. Job cried out for a daysman, an intercessor, and today we know we have that. "For there is one God, and one mediator between God and men, the man Christ Jesus" (1 Tim. 2:5). Now He's the One to whom a great many Christians ought to be going instead of a minister or a psychologist. And if the problem is physical, go to the doctor—and with that go to God also. As Eliphaz could speak from experience, I can also speak from experience and say that God does hear and answer prayer relative to our physical condition and relative to our spiritual condition. It is wonderful to see the way God will deal with Job before He is through with him.

Eliphaz is not going to be very helpful to Job.

Even as I have seen, they that plow iniquity, and sow wickedness, reap the same [Job 4:8].

Eliphaz is speaking from a very high pulpit and is looking down at Job when he says this. He insists there is something hidden in his life which he has not revealed. He is saying that Job is reaping what he sowed.

By the blast of God they perish, and by the breath of his nostrils are they consumed [Job 4:9].

This man is wrong. God disciplines His children, but He never destroys them. Eliphaz is like so many of us who give advice. We can tell someone else how he ought to do things, in a nice way, phrased in very attractive language, but what we say may not be accurate.

The roaring of the lion, and the voice of the fierce lion, and the teeth of the young lions, are broken.

The old lion perisheth for lack of prey, and the stout lion's whelps are scattered abroad [Job 4:10–11].

He is saying that those who sow evil seed are going to reap a harvest of
evil, and they are going to perish like the young lions that have broken
teeth and like the old lions that can no longer stalk their prey.

Now Eliphaz will say that this was impressed on him because he
had a vision. He really tries to make your hair stand on end while he
tells of this dream.

> **Now a thing was secretly brought to me, and mine ear
> received a little thereof [Job 4:12].**

Draw closer now. Cup your ear and don't miss a thing of what is happening.

> **In thoughts from the visions of the night, when deep
> sleep falleth on men,**
>
> **Fear came upon me, and trembling, which made all my
> bones to shake [Job 4:13–14].**

Doesn't this sound mysterious? Isn't it bloodcurdling? The vision
took place at night, in the dark.

> **Then a spirit passed before my face; the hair of my flesh
> stood up:**
>
> **It stood still, but I could not discern the form thereof: an
> image was before mine eyes, there was silence, and I
> heard a voice, saying [Job 4:15–16].**

My, how Eliphaz builds this up! It sounds so scary. It sounds so frightening. This is going to be something nobody's ever heard before. This
is something nobody ever knew before, because this man has had a
vision. He has seen things. He has had a dream. It was dark and a
spirit passed before him. What did it say?

> **Shall mortal man be more just than God? shall a man be
> more pure than his maker? [Job 4:17].**

Now I don't know about you, but I must say I am disappointed. I thought that if a man had had such an experience he was really going to come up with something profound, something that none of us had ever heard before.

This is nothing *new*. I think he really exercised himself a little bit too much to come up with so little. It is like the old saying about the mountain that conceived and travailed and brought forth a mouse! I think that is what Eliphaz did. He's in great travail here, and you expect him to give birth to a great statement, a profound truth. He comes up with this: "Shall a mortal man be more just than God?" Of course not. Any of us knows that, and we didn't need a dream or a frightening nightmare to learn it. I don't think it was worth missing a night's sleep to come up with something so trite, so evident. There is really nothing profound here at all. Yet this is the voice of experience, and there are a lot of folks with the voice of experience today.

I'm in that very difficult spot myself as a retired preacher. Retired preachers can become a nuisance by giving advice—especially to young preachers. When I was young, I can remember how retired preachers would come up, put their arm around me and say, "Son, this is the way you should be doing it." The interesting thing was that they had not done it that way themselves. I find myself doing the same thing now. This very morning I met a young man who is candidating in a church I recommended for him. Before I could even think, I found myself telling him how he ought to do it. Finally I bit my tongue, got back in my car, told him that I would pray for him, and left it there. My, there is a danger in the voice of experience. May I say that Eliphaz was not being helpful to Job.

Let me hasten to say that I don't want to give the impression that Eliphaz and these other men are not stating profound, wonderful truths. The point is that they are not helping Job.

> **Behold, he put no trust in his servants; and his angels he charged with folly:**
>
> **How much less in them that dwell in houses of clay, whose foundation is in the dust, which are crushed before the moth? [Job 4:18–19].**

Even God's angels act rather foolishly. How much more foolish are we who live in houses of clay. There is not a better description of our bodies than that. We live in houses of clay. In 2 Corinthians 5 Paul called our bodies a tent, a feeble, frail tent which the wind will blow over. We live in houses of clay, and before long our houses fall in on us.

> **They are destroyed from morning to evening: they perish for ever without any regarding it.**
>
> **Doth not their excellency which is in them go away? they die, even without wisdom [Job 4:20–21].**

No matter how strong or beautiful our bodies may be, they are of brief duration. Eliphaz is stating truths that are remarkable coming from a period so early in history, but they are not helpful to Job. You see, it is easy to give out truth that is not pertinent, that is not geared into life. We don't need just any truth, but the truth that meets our need.

All of these friends will say some true things, some wonderful things. I enjoy reading this, and I hope you enjoy it. But it doesn't meet the need of Job. One feels like stopping these men and saying, "Don't talk any further because you're going down the wrong road. What you say is not helping this man."

> **Call now, if there be any that will answer thee; and to which the of the saints wilt thou turn? [Job 5:1].**

That is still a good question. To whom will you turn for help? I'm afraid saints are not able to help you. Apparently the patriarchs had already gone on at the time of Job. Probably Abraham and Isaac had died, possibly Jacob was still living. Abraham wasn't able to help; Isaac wasn't able to help—no one who had lived in the past was able to help. Well, which saint are you going to turn to?

> **For wrath killeth the foolish man, and envy slayeth the silly one.**
>
> **I have seen the foolish taking root: but suddenly I cursed his habitation [Job 5:2–3].**

He is saying that he has seen the foolish and the wicked prosper, but finally they are brought down. That, by the way, is true. David was troubled by the prosperity of the wicked and writes, "I have seen the wicked in great power, and spreading himself like a green bay tree. Yet he passed away, and, lo, he was not: yea, I sought him, but he could not be found" (Ps. 37:35–36). David wondered why wicked men prospered while the godly men did not. He watched and noted that finally God brought down the wicked men.

It seemed like a long time before God brought down Hitler and got rid of him. It seemed long while we were living through it, but it was only a few years. Why doesn't God move against evil men today? Well, friend, God moves slowly. God will bring down the ungodly in His own time. He has all eternity ahead of Him.

Eliphaz is classifying Job as one of the foolish ones who took root and was flourishing before he was brought down.

> **His children are far from safety, and they are crushed in the gate, neither is there any to deliver them.**
>
> **Whose harvest the hungry eateth up, and taketh it even out of the thorns, and the robber swalloweth up their substance.**
>
> **Although affliction cometh not forth of the dust, neither doth trouble spring out of the ground;**
>
> **Yet man is born unto trouble, as the sparks fly upward [Job 5:4–7].**

We don't need to pour his last statement into a test tube to find out it is true. Man is born unto trouble. I don't think it is even debatable that the human family has adversity, calamity, sorrow, distress, anxiety, worry, and disturbance. All one needs to do is pick up the newspaper and read a partial report of the human family: fires, accidents, tragedies, wars, rumors of war. The song says, "Nobody knows the trouble I've seen," but really everyone does know because all people have trouble. We do not all have the same color, we are not all the same size, or the same sex, or have the same blood type, or the same I.Q., but we all

have trouble. No one is exempt or immune or can get inoculated for
trouble. Tears are universal. In fact, the word *sympathy* means "to suffer together," and that is the human symphony today—the suffering of
mankind. In fact, a Hebrew word for man is *enash*, meaning "the miserable." That's man. There is nothing sure but death and taxes, we are
told. We can add to this another surety: trouble. "Yet man is born unto
trouble, as the sparks fly upward." The sparks fly upward according to
a universal law, the law of thermodynamics. It isn't by chance or by
luck. The updraft caused by heat on a cool night causes the sparks to
fly upward.

Trouble and suffering and sin are basically the result of disobedi-
ence to God. "There is no peace, saith the LORD, unto the wicked" (Isa.
48:22). Man is trying to build a Utopia in sin, but it won't work. We
cannot have the Millenium without the Prince of Peace. Man is trying
to achieve peace in the world without the Prince of Peace. Therefore
trouble comes to man, and the righteous *do* suffer, and the children of
God *do* have trouble today.

Sometimes trouble comes to a child of God because of a stupid
blunder. A woman once told me, "My husband is my cross." Well, no
matter how bad he is, he is not her cross. She is the one who said yes. It
was her stupid blunder. Your cross is something you take up gladly,
my friend.

Trouble sometimes is a judgment of the Father upon His child. We
are told, ". . . for if we would judge ourselves, we should not be
judged" (1 Cor. 11:31). But if we do not judge ourselves, God will have
to judge us.

Trouble is sometimes a discipline of the Father. We are told in
Scripture, "For whom the Lord loveth he chasteneth, and scourgeth
every son whom he receiveth" (Heb. 12:6). Moses, who was living the
life of Riley in the court of Pharaoh, chose ". . . to suffer affliction with
the people of God, than to enjoy the pleasures of sin for a season"
(Heb. 11:25). It was a discipline for Moses. God could not have used
him as a deliverer if he had not had forty years training down in the
desert of Midian. Also Saul of Tarsus, the proud young Pharisee, came
to know Christ, and God said of him, "For I will shew him how great

things he must suffer for my name's sake" (Acts 9:16). God really put him through the mill! Trouble is a discipline of the Father.

Trouble comes to us sometimes for the purpose of teaching us to be patient and to trust God. Practical James says, "Knowing this, that the trying of your faith worketh patience" (James 1:3).

At other times trouble comes to us because God is putting the sandpaper on us to smooth the rough edges. We will see that Job comes to the realization that God is doing that for him: "But he knoweth the way that I take: when he hath tried me, I shall come forth as gold" (Job 23:10). He saw that God was putting sandpaper on him to smooth him down.

Then sometimes God permits trouble to come to us to get our minds and hearts fastened on Him. This is an explanation, I think, for many of us today.

There are good reasons, my friend, for trouble coming to a child of God. Therefore Eliphaz is accurate when he says, "Yet man is born unto trouble, as the sparks fly upward."

> **I would seek unto God, and unto God would I commit my cause:**
>
> **Which doeth great things and unsearchable; marvellous things without number:**
>
> **Who giveth rain upon the earth, and sendeth waters upon the fields:**
>
> **To set up on high those that be low; that those which mourn may be exalted to safety.**
>
> **He disappointeth the devices of the crafty, so that their hands cannot perform their enterprise.**
>
> **He taketh the wise in their own craftiness: and the counsel of the froward is carried headlong.**
>
> **They meet with darkness in the daytime, and grope in the noonday as in the night.**

> **But he saveth the poor from the sword, from their mouth, and from the hand of the mighty.**
>
> **So the poor hath hope, and iniquity stoppeth her mouth [Job 5:8–16].**

What he is saying here—and he is saying it really in a beautiful way—is that God is faithful and God is good and God is just. While this is true, it doesn't reach the root of the problem of this man Job. Eliphaz actually is not even talking to Job.

> **Behold, happy is the man whom God correcteth: therefore despise not thou the chastening of the Almighty [Job 5:17].**

I have heard this verse quoted again and again. Isn't it true? Of course it is true, but Eliphaz was using it as a personal dig against Job. Chastening is not always the reason that God's people suffer, as we have seen. Sometimes one can use this verse as a little dagger to put into the heart of a friend. It is a nice way of saying, "You are having trouble because you've done wrong and God is correcting you." Well, that could be, but it may not be. Who are you to make such a judgment? Do you have a telephone into heaven? Has the Lord revealed some secret to you? There are people who like to speak *ex cathedra*, and they are not even the Pope! Some people think they have the last word on everything. Listen, friend, you cannot always speak to the problem of someone else, and someone else cannot always speak to your problem either. Although the statement of Eliphaz is true, it does not apply to Job.

> **For he maketh sore, and bindeth up: he woundeth, and his hands make whole [Job 5:18].**

What a wonderful picture of God that is.

> **He shall deliver thee in six troubles; yea, in seven there shall no evil touch thee [Job 5:19].**

You will notice this use of seven again in Proverbs 6:16 and, in fact, quite often throughout the Bible. It is not just a poetic expression. It means seven—not the number of perfection—the number of completeness. For instance, the seventh day was the completion of one week. Seven is the number of completeness here, as he gives the total spectrum of the trouble of man.

> **In famine he shall redeem thee from death: and in war from the power of the sword.**

> **Thou shalt be hid from the scourge of the tongue: neither shalt thou be afraid of destruction when it cometh [Job 5:20-21].**

God will deliver you in these seven troubles: (1) In famine he shall redeem thee from death, (2) in war from the power of the sword, (3) from the scourge of the tongue. During the war in Vietnam we were given a body count in the daily news. I wonder what the body count from gossip would be in this day. The tongue has probably killed more people than war has. We need to pray that God will deliver us from the evil tongue. A woman in a church I served had a very evil tongue. I remember praying, "Oh God, don't let her hit me with that tongue." I found out that she did use her tongue against me. She was mean, but God protected me from being hurt by her. (4) God will deliver from the fear of destruction when it cometh—that is the typhoon, the tornado, the storm. When I was a boy, it seemed like I spent half my life in a storm cellar in West Texas. God did deliver us, but He expected us to go to the storm cellars.

> **At destruction and famine thou shalt laugh: neither shalt thou be afraid of the beasts of the earth [Job 5:22].**

(5) He delivers from famine. Have you ever stopped to think that generally wherever the Gospel has gone, whether or not it has been widely accepted, you find one of the prosperous areas of the world? These nations are the "haves." I do not think that is an accident. I have often

thought that with the food we send to "have not" countries should be prizes like we get in boxes of Crackerjacks. And the prize should be the Word of God. Blessing attends the reading of the Word. (6) Neither shalt thou be afraid of the beasts of the earth.

> For thou shalt be in league with the stones of the field: and the beasts of the field shall be at peace with thee.

> And thou shalt know that thy tabernacle shall be in peace; and thou shalt visit thy habitation, and shalt not sin.

> Thou shalt know also that thy seed shall be great, and thine offspring as the grass of the earth.

> Thou shalt come to thy grave in a full age, like as a shock of corn cometh in his season [Job 5:23–26].

(7) The last trouble is death. Eliphaz speaks of death, not as an awful hideous monster, but as something welcome. There is a leveling out in death.

> Lo this, we have searched it, so it is; hear it, and know thou it for thy good [Job 5:27].

This concludes the first discourse of Eliphaz. It has not met the need of Job. It hasn't touched him at all. As a matter of fact, Job is dismayed; he is alarmed, and he cries out for pity. He cries out for mercy and for help because Eliphaz was of no help to him at all.

CHAPTERS 6 AND 7

THEME: *Job's answer to Eliphaz*

But Job answered and said,

Oh that my grief were throughly weighed, and my calamity laid in the balances together! [Job 6:1–2].

Job is making a plaintive plea. He says, "I can't even tell you how terrible my grief is. I can't explain to you this awful thing that has happened to me." You can see that Eliphaz had not helped him at all. Just to say, "You have some secret sin and the thing for you to do now is to confess and get right with God," is not always the correct thing to say. Job is saying, "You need to recognize what my question is." Eliphaz had missed the point altogether. He said a lot of nice things, good things, true things, but he didn't help Job. It is like giving the answer, "Christ is the answer," when you don't know what the question is.

Job needs more than has been given him by Eliphaz. He is crying out like a wounded animal.

For now it would be heavier than the sand of the sea: therefore my words are swallowed up.

For the arrows of the Almighty are within me, the poison whereof drinketh up my spirit: the terrors of God do set themselves in array against me.

Doth the wild ass bray when he hath grass? or loweth the ox over his fodder? [Job 6:3–5].

Job says, "I am crying out and you can see my misery and you show no pity at all. You act as if I'm not in trouble. I wouldn't be crying out if I weren't." He points out that the long-eared donkey out in the field doesn't bray for something to eat when he is eating grass. So Job is

saying that he wouldn't be crying out if there were nothing hurting him. He says, "I'm hurting and I'm hurting bad."

> **Can that which is unsavoury be eaten without salt? or is there any taste in the white of an egg?**

> **The things that my soul refused to teach are as my sorrowful meat [Job 6:6–7].**

"Sorrowful meat" is loathsome food.

> **Oh that I might have my request; and that God would grant me the thing that I long for!**

> **Even that it would please God to destroy me; that he would let loose his hand, and cut me off! [Job 6:8–9].**

He has hit bottom. He finds no help anywhere. He actually questions the justice of God. He is miserable. He wishes God would destroy him, get rid of him, let loose His hand, and cut him off. He wants to die.

> **Then should I yet have comfort; yea, I would harden myself in sorrow: let him not spare; for I have not concealed the words of the Holy One.**

> **What is my strength, that I should hope? and what is mine end, that I should prolong my life? [Job 6:10–11].**

He is saying, "I have nothing to live for."

> **Is my strength the strength of stones? or is my flesh of brass? [Job 6:12].**

"I am weary. I can't stand any more."

> **Is not my help in me? and is wisdom driven quite from me? [Job 6:13].**

Now listen to his cry.

> **To him that is afflicted pity should be shewed from his friend; but he forsaketh the fear of the Almighty [Job 6:14].**

My friend should have shown pity, should have sympathized with me. But he didn't.

> **My brethren have dealt deceitfully as a brook, and as the stream of brooks they pass away [Job 6:15].**

The meaning in the Hebrew is that they were like a mirage in the desert.

This is beautiful, poetic language. It is as if he says that he looked down the road and saw his three friends coming and said to himself, *Oh thank God, here come my friends. They will understand me and they will sympathize with me.* Their sympathy would be like an oasis in the desert, but it was only a mirage.

> **Which are blackish by reason of the ice, and wherein the snow is hid:**
>
> **What time they wax warm, they vanish: when it is hot, they are consumed out of their place [Job 6:16–17].**

He says they are like a pool that is covered with ice and snow. It is deceitful. You think you can walk on it, but when you step on it, you fall through. That is the type of friends they have turned out to be.

What a picture Job gives us!

I'm not sure but what Job's cry is the cry of the human predicament in our day. Man with all his comforts and his gadgets—oh, how lonesome, how restless, how unhappy he is! He is *Enash*, the miserable one. He needs more than gadgets; he needs *God*.

Now Job will say, "If you have something to tell me, *tell* me. I'm teachable."

> Teach me, and I will hold my tongue: and cause me to
> understand wherein I have erred.
>
> How forcible are right words! but what doth your argu-
> ing reprove?
>
> Do ye imagine to reprove words, and the speeches of one
> that is desperate, which are as wind? [Job 6:24–26].

He says, "What you have said is good, but it doesn't touch my case at
all. You're not diagnosing my condition."

I heard of a person who went to a doctor, and his case was diagnosed as arthritis. It turned out to be a cancer, but by the time the
patient got into the hands of a cancer specialist, it was too late to do
anything for him. That is the problem of Job. He says, "You have come
and you have attempted to diagnose my case, but your diagnosis is
wrong. You have said it is hidden sin, and it isn't that at all. Now if you
diagnose it accurately and you have something helpful to say to me,
say it and I'll listen to you."

Remember that these three friends didn't really know God, they
didn't really know Job, and they didn't really know themselves. They
didn't understand the true situation, and all three will come to the
conclusion that Job had sinned and won't confess the truth. Since he
won't confess his secret sin, he is being judged.

> Is there not an appointed time to man upon earth? are
> not his days also like the days of an hireling?
>
> As a servant earnestly desireth the shadow, and as an
> hireling looketh for the reward of his work:
>
> So am I made to possess months of vanity, and weari-
> some nights are appointed to me [Job 7:1–3].

Job has no relief from his sorrow or from his pain. He is a very sick
man, and his friends seem to ignore that. They had not offered him any
comfort. Even his wife, his helpmeet, has suggested suicide to him.

When his world caved in, he became a distraught and frustrated man
to be pitied.

> **When I lie down, I say, When shall I arise, and the
> nights be gone? and I am full of tossings to and fro unto
> the dawning of the day.**

> **My flesh is clothed with worms and clods of dust; my
> skin is broken, and become loathsome.**

> **My days are swifter than a weaver's shuttle, and are
> spent without hope [Job 7:4–6].**

Job apparently felt he had an incurable disease and that the end was
coming and was not far off. He probably did have such a disease. In all
this his friends paid no attention to his problem. They have come to
him but have not ministered to his need. They just didn't understand.
It has been said that a friend is one who knows you and *still* loves you.
These friends didn't really know Job. He says that at least his physical
condition should have called forth some sympathy from them.

> **When I say, My bed shall comfort me, my couch shall
> ease my complaint;**

> **Then thou scarest me with dreams, and terrifiest me
> through visions:**

> **So that my soul chooseth strangling, and death rather
> than my life.**

> **I loathe it; I would not live alway: let me alone; for my
> days are vanity [Job 7:13–16].**

It seems that his fever drove him to periods of delirium and hallucina-
tions.

> **What is man, that thou shouldest magnify him? and that
> thou shouldest set thine heart upon him?**

> **And that thou shouldest visit him every morning, and try him every moment?**
>
> **How long wilt thou not depart from me, nor let me alone till I swallow down my spittle? [Job 7:17–19].**

He wishes he could just die in peace. He wishes that God would let him alone. He senses that he is being tried, but he hasn't any notion what is really behind all of this.

His reaction is the reaction of many. "Just leave me alone in my misery."

> **I have sinned; what shall I do unto thee, O thou preserver of men? why hast thou set me as a mark against thee, so that I am a burden to myself?**
>
> **And why dost thou not pardon my transgression, and take away mine iniquity? for now shall I sleep in the dust; and thou shalt seek me in the morning, but I shall not be [Job 7:20–21].**

They have raised the question of Job's sin. Job doesn't claim to be guiltless. He admits he has sinned. But why should he be selected for this special attack as a notorious sinner? Why should his life be a burden when he is not that kind of a sinner? Why doesn't God show mercy on him? Why doesn't God pardon his sin and restore him?

While he admits that he is a sinner, he says that he is getting more than he deserves.

We can see in Job a breaking down of his integrity. When a man's integrity is broken down, he becomes an easy mark for Satan. This is the thing that happens to many a man today who attempts to fight life alone. He begins to hit the bottle or he drops into sin. Satan has a chance to attack him because the man's integrity has broken down. This is the situation with Job. Will Job break under all of this?

CHAPTER 8

THEME: *Bildad's first discourse*

The next man who makes his attack upon Job is Bildad. He is what we would call a traditionalist. Bildad is a man who rests upon the past. His argument is: "For inquire, I pray thee, of the former age, and prepare thyself to the search of their fathers" (Job 8:8). It is as if he picks up the old rocks and stones of geology, looks at them and tells what happened years ago and from them predicts what will happen.

Actually, the evolutionist is really a traditionalist, which a great many people do not recognize. The evolutionist rests upon the past and assumes certain premises which he cannot prove. There are only two explanations for the origin of this universe: one is creation and the other is speculation. Evolution is speculation. It digs up a bone, attempts to date it and classify it as belonging to a certain period, and then relate it to the development of man. But who knows? This Book of Job is going to raise that very question. In Job 38:4 God asks Job, "Where wast thou when I laid the foundations of the earth? declare, if thou hast understanding." Bildad will use the argument of "when I was young," and "we've been doing it this way." He knew a lot of old sayings and proverbs and pious platitudes, but he actually offers nothing new at all. He is a more crude fellow than Eliphaz. He breaks in upon Job and hurts him a great deal. He doesn't help Job at all. This is Bildad who is supposed to have been his friend.

BILDAD RESTS HIS ARGUMENT ON TRADITION

Then answered Bildad the Shuhite, and said,

How long wilt thou speak these things? and how long shall the words of thy mouth be like a strong wind? [Job 8:1–2].

These men really get in some good ones. This is real repartee. This is a real rap session they are having here. They are brilliant men, by the way. Notice that Bildad puts the knife into Job and twists it a little. He says, "Job, listening to you is just like listening to the wind blowing. You're a windy individual." Actually, I would say they are all a little windy, including Job. We will see a little later that there is something wrong with Job, too.

So this remark by Bildad was good for a laugh at the expense of Job. A crowd had gathered around by this time. This was as interesting to people as a football game or a basketball game would be today. They were interested in an intellectual contest as we seem to be interested in physical contests. I wonder who are the more civilized people!

> **Doth God pervert judgment? or doth the Almighty pervert justice? [Job 8:3].**

He is really saying, "Job, you are getting exactly what you had coming to you. You try to defend yourself, but it means that there is some great sin in your life and you are getting exactly what you deserve."

> **If thy children have sinned against him, and he have cast them away for their transgression [Job 8:4].**

Now that is an awful thing to say. He is suggesting that the reason Job's children were destroyed was because they were sinners. I can't think of anything anyone could say that would hurt more than that. Bildad had no right to say that. We know (because God let us in on it from the beginning of the book) that his children were not destroyed for that reason.

> **If thou wouldest seek unto God betimes, and make thy supplication to the Almighty;**
>
> **If thou wert pure and upright; surely now he would awake for thee, and make the habitation of thy righteousness prosperous [Job 8:5–6].**

Job, if you were lily white, as you have given the impression, God would hear your prayer and heal and restore you. But as it is, there must be something radically wrong.

Though thy beginning was small, yet thy latter end should greatly increase [Job 8:7].

By the way, that is what is going to happen. When all of this is over, Job will greatly increase—God is going to double everything he had.

For inquire, I pray thee, of the former age, and prepare thyself to the search of their fathers [Job 8:8].

Bildad is going back to the old evolutionary theory. He is going to say that everything works according to set laws. He will put down quite a few of those laws which are old sayings.

(For we are but of yesterday, and know nothing, because our days upon earth are a shadow:) [Job 8:9].

"We are but of yesterday and know nothing" is a true statement. Of course, Bildad doesn't really feel that *he* knows nothing; he means that Job knows nothing. However, the statement was true of Bildad, it is true of the evolutionists, and it is true of you and me. We are but of yesterday. Man is a "Johnny-come-lately" in God's universe. He hasn't been around very long. God has not seen fit to tell us what He was doing back in the millenniums before man arrived on the scene. Frankly, I'm not interested in the eternity past, but I am very interested in what He is going to be doing in the millions of years from today, because I expect to be around then.

Shall not they teach thee, and tell thee, and utter words out of their heart? [Job 8:10].

Bildad says that the past will teach us. Men try to take a few rocks and a few bones and then pretend they know all about the origin of the

earth and its development. May I say to you that man is assuming more than he could possibly know.

Notice how different is the philosophy of the apostle Paul. He pointed to Christ and to the future: "I press toward the mark for the prize of the high calling of God in Christ Jesus" (Phil 3:14). The only way we can learn about eternal things is from the Word of God.

Now Bildad gets more candid and more crude.

> **Can the rush grow up without mire? can the flag grow without water?**
>
> **Whilst it is yet in his greenness, and not cut down, it withereth before any other herb [Job 8:11–12].**

He tries to get very scientific here, but any third grader would know the answer. I've learned the answer here in California. I need to water my flags out by my back fence or they will not grow. That is not very profound wisdom. Who doesn't know this!

> **So are the paths of all that forget God; and the hypocrite's hope shall perish [Job 8:13].**

Now he is accusing Job of being a hypocrite! He says Job has been covering up something. He says to Job, "You've been a hypocrite, just putting up a front."

> **Whose hope shall be cut off, and whose trust shall be a spider's web.**
>
> **He shall lean upon his house, but it shall not stand: he shall hold it fast, but it shall not endure [Job 8:14–15].**

That's as good as leaning on a spider's web. When trouble comes, it won't hold you.

> **Behold, God will not cast away a perfect man, neither will he help the evildoers [Job 8:20].**

Now, wait a minute—is that actually true? God has certainly helped me although I have been an evildoer. He saved me, my friend. Will God "cast away a perfect man"? No, He won't. But where is the perfect man? There is none. The Scripture is clear on that score: ". . . There is none righteous, no, not one" (Rom. 3:10). Although what Bildad says is true, it is not true when you pour it into the test tube of life and pour the acid of experience upon it.

> **Till he fill thy mouth with laughing, and thy lips with rejoicing.**

> **They that hate thee shall be clothed with shame; and the dwelling place of the wicked shall come to nought [Job 8:21–22].**

He is telling Job that he has come to nothing because he is a great sinner. That is not very helpful for a man who is in the position of Job! You see, Bildad does not know God. He does not know Job. Neither does he really know himself. He is a traditionalist. He thinks that by scientific examination he can tell you how the world began. He is a smart boy, but he doesn't know. He cannot put himself in the place of God.

In the following chapter we will see that Job answers Bildad, and he does it very well, although he is getting awfully weary of these rounds of conversation.

CHAPTERS 9 AND 10

THEME: Job's answer to Bildad

Job makes it very clear that Bildad has not met his need at all. He was not even talking in the field of his problem. At this point he makes it clear that he makes no claim to perfection, and he knows that he cannot defend himself before God. What he needs is someone on his side to present his case. We will hear Job's longing for someone to be his mediator and his intercessor. In other words, we will hear Job's heart-cry for Christ.

> **Then Job answered and said,**
>
> **I know it is so of a truth: but how should man be just with God? [Job 9:1–2].**

That is, much of what Bildad had said is true. The problem is that his words haven't met the need of Job, they haven't spoken to the problem of Job. "I know that in a general way your words are true," says Job, "but the question is 'How can I be just with God?'"

Job surely needed the gospel at this point. He needed to know how a man could be just with God. Job says he wants some questions answered, and his friends are not answering the questions.

> **If he will contend with him, he cannot answer him one of a thousand.**
>
> **He is wise in heart, and mighty in strength: who hath hardened himself against him and hath prospered? [Job 9:3–4].**

Job says, "I don't pretend. If you think I am trying to put up a front before God, you are wrong. I know I cannot contend with Him. He could ask me a question and I would never be able to answer." Job

wants an answer to his questions, and he wants God to answer him. God is far removed from him.

> **Which removeth the mountains, and they know not: which overturneth them in his anger.**

> **Which shaketh the earth out of her place, and the pillars thereof tremble.**

> **Which commandeth the sun, and it riseth not; and sealeth up the stars.**

> **Which alone spreadeth out the heavens, and treadeth upon the waves of the sea [Job 9:5–8].**

Here is a tremendous picture of God as the Creator. Job knows Him as the Creator but knows nothing about His tender mercy at this time.

> **Which maketh Arcturus, Orion, and Pleiades, and the chambers of the south.**

> **Which doeth great things past finding out; yea, and wonders without number [Job 9:9–10].**

We can see that Job knew something about the stars. However, he is not attempting to say that he is in the situation of his misery because he was born under a certain star. That is without a doubt one of the most foolish things men say. Shakespeare had the answer to that when Mark Antony said, "The fault, dear Brutus, is not in our stars, But in our selves, that we are underlings." Job knew the stars did not account for his situation. He recognized God as the Creator of the stars.

> **Lo, he goeth by me, and I see him not: he passeth on also, but I perceive him not [Job 9:11].**

Job knows God as the Creator of the universe, and he also knows God is a spirit, and Job cannot see Him at all.

> **If God will not withdraw his anger, the proud helpers do stoop under him.**
>
> **How much less shall I answer him, and choose out my words to reason with him? [Job 9:13–14].**

Job knows that he wouldn't stand a chance if he came into the presence of God. If God should speak to him, he wouldn't know what to answer.

> **If I had called, and he had answered me; yet would I not believe that he had hearkened unto my voice [Job 9:16].**

Job couldn't believe that He was really listening to him.

> **For he breaketh me with a tempest, and multiplieth my wounds without cause.**
>
> **He will not suffer me to take my breath, but filleth me with bitterness.**
>
> **If I speak of strength, lo, he is strong: and if of judgment, who shall set me a time to plead? [Job 9:17–19].**

Job asks, "How in the world can I plead my case before Him?"

> **If I justify myself, mine own mouth shall condemn me: if I say, I am perfect, it shall also prove me perverse [Job 9:20].**

Job says, "If I try to pretend I am perfect, my own mouth will condemn me." However, we will find later on that Job has a high estimation of himself. He is not the man who said, "For I know that in me (that is, in my flesh,) dwelleth no good thing . . ." (Rom. 7:18). Job does not say that he is a perfect man before God, but he does contend that he is a pretty good man—in fact, a righteous man. Yet he recognizes that before God he would not be able to defend himself.

There are many men today who, because they do not know the

Word of God, feel that they will be able to stand before God and meet His standards and will actually be well-pleasing to Him.

I remember an oilman in Nashville, Tennessee. He was one of a group of businessmen with whom I used to play volleyball three times a week. He was a godless man although he was a church member. He and I were always on opposite sides, and he didn't like me to beat him. One night he had really been beaten, so he began to argue with me in the locker room. He said, "I heard you speak (I had a morning devotion on the radio in those days) about a religion that calls men sinners who need to come to Christ. I don't believe that stuff. I believe in helping people. In my business I give men jobs. I pay them money so they can buy beans to put on their tables. I think that is better than any religion you have to offer." How do you answer a man like that before a group of men all gathered in the locker room? Some of the men were church members, but most of them were godless and unsaved men. It was difficult to know how to answer that—until about a year later when we were in the locker room and that man was not there. He was in jail. He had been arrested for the way he had been conducting his business. He defrauded not only the government but also his own employees. I shall never forget that another of the men mentioned his name and said, "Well, I don't think he'd have much of a chance before God. He didn't do so well before Judge So-and-So the other day. They found out he really wasn't putting beans on the plates of his employees, but he was really taking them off their plates." That really shook those men. Very candidly, I saw several of them in my church services, and I even had the privilege of leading one of those men to the Lord. But the point is that men have a misconception of God. They think they are good enough to stand before Him. Job is saying in effect, "If I come into God's presence, He will think of something in me that I am not aware of, and I won't be able to answer Him."

JOB'S HEART-CRY FOR CHRIST

For he is not a man, as I am, that I should answer him, and we should come together in judgment [Job 9:32].

Job is saying in effect, "If He were a *man*, I could talk to Him." This is the reason God became a Man, my friend—so man could talk to Him and walk with Him and realize that he cannot meet God's standards. The only Man who ever met God's standards was the Lord Jesus Christ.

This is what makes some of the contemporary plays and literature such a curse. They insinuate that Jesus was not only a man, but that He was a sinful man! Liberalism has been saying this for years. However, they cannot find in the Word of God that there was any sin in the Lord Jesus Christ. They find the sin in their own dirty hearts because Jesus was without sin.

Because Jesus was a Man, I can go to Him. He died for me on the cross! And He shows me by His life that I cannot meet God's standards, that I need a Savior. By His death He can save me. This is what poor old Job was longing for.

> **Neither is there any daysman betwixt us, that might lay his hand upon us both [Job 9:33].**

Job's complaint was that there was no mediator between him and God. His cry is this: "Oh, if there were only Someone who could put His hand in the hand of God and who could put His other hand in my hand and bring us together. If He could do that, then I would have a mediator." In the New Testament Paul wrote to a young preacher, "For there is one God, and one mediator between God and men, the man Christ Jesus" (1 Tim. 2:5).

The song that says, "Put your hand in the hand of the Man from Galilee" is only half true. The Man of Galilee has another hand, and that hand is the hand of God. Jesus is God, my friend; He is the God-Man. What a glorious, wonderful truth that is. Oh, how Job longed for Him!

> **My soul is weary of my life; I will leave my complaint upon myself; I will speak in the bitterness of my soul [Job 10:1].**

Because Job has no mediator, no man to represent him before God, he will just speak in the bitterness of his soul. He is weary of life, and he is going to say exactly how he feels. He is plain and honest about his sad plight and his wretched condition.

> **I will say unto God, Do not condemn me; shew me wherefore thou contendest with me [Job 10:2].**

God is going to answer him on this before we are through the book. God is going to show Job something about himself, something that all of us need to find out about ourselves.

> **Is it good unto thee that thou shouldest oppress, that thou shouldest despise the work of thine hands, and shine upon the counsel of the wicked? [Job 10:3].**

Job cannot understand why he must suffer so while there are wicked men who are not suffering. By the way, that was the problem that confronted David. That is a problem that has confronted me. As a pastor I have wondered sometimes why God would let certain wonderful, godly men suffer while at the same time godless men—even men in the church—seemed to get by with sin. They seem to get by with it for a time, but I notice that in time God deals with these people. Even so, there are times when we all ask this question. You see, this book faces up to the questions of life. It is right down where the rubber meets the road.

> **Hast thou eyes of flesh? or seest thou as man seeth? [Job 10:4].**

Job bewails his condition and his sad plight. He wonders whether God really sees him in his true condition.

Here is another reason that God became a man down here: now I have the assurance that there is a Man in the Glory who understands me. Because He was a Man like I am, He knows exactly how I feel.

There is not a pulsation that ever entered the human breast that Jesus Christ did not feel when He was here on this earth. My friend, He knows how I feel. He knows how you feel.

> **Are thy days as the days of man? are thy years as man's days,**
>
> **That thou inquirest after mine iniquity, and searchest after my sin?**
>
> **Thou knowest that I am not wicked; and there is none that can deliver out of thine hand [Job 10:5–7].**

Job now begins to defend himself. He is not willing to admit that there is a great sin in his life. He says that he finds himself in a pretty awkward situation. "God knows that I am not wicked, and yet I cannot get out of His hand. I must go through all this—and I don't see why I should be put through this."

Job was a man who needed a little humility, and God is going to give him that humility. Have you ever noticed that humility and patience are qualities that God doesn't hand over to you on a silver platter with a silver spoon for you to lap up? You don't become humble that way. Patience and humility are fruit of the Holy Spirit produced in your life through trying experiences. God is going to produce both humility and patience in this man Job.

In the New Testament we hear about the patience of Job. James writes, ". . . Ye have heard of the patience of Job," but he also adds, "and have seen the end of the Lord; that the Lord is very pitiful, and of tender mercy" (James 5:11). It wasn't that Job was naturally a patient man—that quality would have increased his self-confidence and his conceit. Actually Job was not patient. We have seen that his patience broke down, and he is crying out to God in impatience. But when we see the "end of the Lord," that is, the outcome of the Lord's dealing with him, then we see that God was *making* him patient, and God was *giving* him humility. It is God who does this, you see.

I should have been as though I had not been: I should have been carried from the womb to the grave [Job 10:19].

Job is back at the thing he started with and will stay with it part of the way through this book. During this time of testing, death was something that he desired. He felt that death would put him out of his misery. It would get him away from this scene. He would welcome it as sleep, as something that would put him in a place of unconsciousness.

Now if you think you can draw something from this book to sustain the doctrine of soul sleep, you are entirely wrong. Job will say before we get through this book, "For I know that my redeemer liveth . . . yet in my flesh shall I see God" (Job 19:25–26). My friend, this book does not teach soul sleep at all.

But at this point, Job is wishing that he had never been born. He wishes for complete oblivion. That is something you can wish for, too. Job was not the only one who did that. Elijah wished it. Jonah wished it. The only thing is, it won't do you one bit of good. To wish you hadn't been born is a complete waste of time. And, by the way, wishing you were dead won't help either. No one ever died by wishing. I always suspect that most of us who say we wish we were dead don't really mean it. We are just talking. When people face death, they really want to live. I suspect that if Job had really faced up to it, he didn't really mean he wished he were dead either. But right now he is pouring out his soul, and there is a breaking down of the dignity of this man. God is going to need to get through to his heart.

A lot of God's saints today have proud, hard hearts. Sometimes God must deal with us as He dealt with Job.

CHAPTER 11

THEME: *Zophar's first discourse*

Now we meet the last of Job's friends. His name is Zophar, and he is the legalist. He assumed (and rightly so as far as he goes) that God works according to measure, according to law. He pretends to know what God will do in a given circumstance.

He is different from Bildad, who was the traditionalist. Bildad said you can go back and look at what has happened in the past and learn from it. He had a scientific mind. He is like the scientist who thinks he can look at rocks and tell you how old the earth is. Zophar had a scientific mind, too, but he puts the emphasis on the laws. If one would bring him up to date, he would be more or less an atheist. His philosophy is that the universe is run by laws. It is obvious that we cannot have law without somebody who makes the law. Nevertheless, Zophar assumes this physical universe is following laws.

Zophar is like the fellow who says, "Ask me another." He is the I-have-all-the-answers type. He is the voice of legalism. He holds that God is bound by laws and never operates beyond the circumference of His own laws. He is probably the senior member of the group, and he speaks with a dogmatic finality that is even more candid and crude than that of Bildad.

Then answered Zophar the Naamathite, and said,

Should not the multitude of words be answered? and should a man full of talk be justified? [Job 11:1–2].

He is saying that Job is covering his sin with words. Job has tried to make it clear that a man in his condition—suffering as he is—is not apt to put up a front. Zophar simply ignores that and says that Job is trying to talk his way out of his situation. It is true that there are men who are able to talk their way out of a situation and who are clever at manipula-

tion by words. That is the way some lawyers win cases in court. It is really not a matter of justice being done but rather the cleverness of the lawyer and his manipulation. This is not true of Job.

> **Should thy lies make men hold their peace? and when thou mockest, shall no man make thee ashamed? [Job 11:3].**

Zophar goes a step farther and actually accuses Job of lying. "Should thy lies make men hold their peace?" He has accused him of being a hypocrite, and now he accuses him of lying. That is even more crude than Bildad had been. Bildad had said that Job was a hypocrite but had never called him a liar.

Zophar is now going to assume the pious position of being on the inside with God. He thinks he knows what God will do under a certain circumstance. Of course, while he is on the inside with God, Job is on the outside, unable to know what God is doing. So Zophar feels that Job ought to listen to him because he has the final word and that his word is, in fact, the word of God.

> **For thou hast said, My doctrine is pure, and I am clean in thine eyes.**
>
> **But oh that God would speak, and open his lips against thee [Job 11:4–5].**

Since God wasn't speaking, Zophar speaks for Him.

I received a rather crude letter the other day. It was from a man who was rebuking me for a position that I held, which to him indicated I was not only a very ignorant and dogmatic man, but that I had no spiritual discernment whatsoever. Then he proceeded to give me his interpretation. When he finished, he said, "Now I am going to see whether you will listen to the Holy Spirit or not." Isn't that interesting? That man claimed to be the voice of the Holy Spirit. If I didn't listen to him, it meant I wasn't listening to God.

As I read his letter, I felt confident that he was totally unaware of the fact that he was doing the very thing he had accused me of doing!

Supposing the man did have some inside information that I do not have access to, he certainly was not proceeding in a way that was helpful to me. In fact, his letter was not at all helpful to me and ended up in the "round file," which is the wastebasket. I put it there because it had no message for me.

I don't think Zophar had a message for Job.

> **And that he would shew thee the secrets of wisdom, that they are double to that which is! Know therefore that God exacteth of thee less than thine iniquity deserveth [Job 11:6].**

And what he says to Job is really a blow, not a comfort. He tells Job that he is not even getting half of what he really has coming to him. Now that is a pretty hard statement. He says the fact that Job is suffering as much as he is shows that Job is a lot worse than his friends even dreamed he was.

Zophar is not very helpful to a man in Job's condition! We must remember that all this time Job is a sick man and is in desperate pain. He actually thinks he may expire at any moment and at times he hopes that he will die.

> **Canst thou by searching find out God? canst thou find out the Almighty unto perfection? [Job 11:7].**

That is a great statement. It is a marvelous statement. But who doesn't know that? Job will tell him later that everyone knows that. No man can *discover* God; God is *revealed*. The only way you can know about God is what He is pleased to reveal of Himself to us. I have come to the conclusion that He has revealed very little of Himself to us. In fact, the little that He has revealed to us has some of us so awestruck and some so confused that we can see why He hasn't revealed more of Himself to us.

You cannot "find out God" by starting out like a Columbus in search of Him. Nor can you find God by going into space in a sputnik. I recall that the Russians published in their paper the fact that they

hadn't discovered God in the early days of space exploration, and so they assumed He was not there. We can put little gadgets out in space, but they won't find God. To think they could find Him is absurd!

Man cannot look through a microscope or out into the heavens through a telescope and discover God. God must reveal Himself to man. This is a profound statement that Zophar makes, but it is nothing new to Job.

> **It is as high as heaven; what canst thou do? deeper than hell; what canst thou know?**
>
> **The measure thereof is longer than the earth, and broader than the sea [Job 11:8–9].**

He gives a lofty discourse about God which is tremendous. It just doesn't touch the need of Job.

> **If he cut off, and shut up, or gather together, then who can hinder him?**
>
> **For he knoweth vain men; he seeth wickedness also; will he not then consider it?**
>
> **For vain man would be wise, though man be born like a wild ass's colt [Job 11:10–12].**

Of course, he is speaking of Job here—not of himself! He feels that he is the man who has the answer.

> **If thou prepare thine heart, and stretch out thine hands toward him;**
>
> **If iniquity be in thine hand, put it far away, and let not wickedness dwell in thy tabernacles [Job 11:13–14].**

Again he comes at Job on the basis that Job is hiding something, that there is secret sin in Job's life. All three of Job's friends assume that Job

is covering up something. Job actually isn't aware of anything that he should put away; yet there is something, as we shall see later.

> **For then shalt thou lift up thy face without spot; yea, thou shalt be stedfast, and shalt not fear:**

> **Because thou shalt forget thy misery, and remember it as waters that pass away:**

> **And thine age shall be clearer than the noonday; thou shalt shine forth, thou shalt be as the morning [Job 11:15–17].**

Zophar is saying, "If you would just deal with the sin that is in your life and quit fighting it, God would hear and answer your prayers and restore you."

> **But the eyes of the wicked shall fail, and they shall not escape, and their hope shall be as the giving up of the ghost [Job 11:20].**

He concludes by saying to Job, "You are going to come to the time when the judgment of God will be upon you unless you confess your secret sin." He predicts the absolute and complete judgment of Job.

That concludes Zophar's address which in reality is an attack upon Job. All three friends have now had their little say. Job's answer will be one of the lengthiest discourses in the book.

CHAPTERS 12—14

THEME: Job replies to his three friends

This lengthy reply that Job makes in this section concludes the first round of discourses. Remember that in Job's day folk enjoyed intellectual competition—men pitting their minds against each other. Today it is not brain but brawn in athletic contests.

> **And Job answered and said,**
>
> **No doubt but ye are the people, and wisdom shall die with you [Job 12:1–2].**

Now there is a sarcastic statement and a pretty good one. Job says, "You fellows think you have all the answers. You are *the* people, and wisdom will die with you!" They were talking as if Job were a simpleton and they had all the answers.

> **But I have understanding as well as you; I am not inferior to you: yea, who knoweth not such things as these? [Job 12:3].**

Job knows as much as they know. The problem is that they have not spoken to the situation as it really is. There is something important in these discourses that I want to call to your attention so you can be watching for it. Instead of leading Job to self-judgment, the three friends only minister to a spirit of self-vindication in Job. In other words, they make an attack on Job which forces him to come back with a defense of himself.

They did not introduce God into the scene. They did not speak of a God of mercy and a God of grace, but a God of law. Although He is a God of law, He is also a God of grace and mercy. They brought in experience and tradition and legality, but they didn't bring in *the truth*.

When they brought their incriminations against Job, it caused him to defend himself and to declare that he was right. The minute Job started justifying himself he was not justifying God. Up to this point it looks as if Job is saying that God is wrong and that God is the One to be criticized.

This is a position which many people take today, even many Christian people. The friends should have led Job to condemn himself and to vindicate God. God has recorded all these discourses in His Word to reveal this truth. The utterances of Job will prove how far he was from that true brokenness of spirit and humility of mind which flows from being in the divine Presence. His friends never brought him to the place where he said as Paul said, "For I know that in me (that is, in my flesh) dwelleth no good thing," (Rom. 7:18) or, ". . . by the grace of God I am what I am" (1 Cor. 15:10).

There are too many Christians today who boast of who they are and what they have done and how much they give. It looks as if God is on the receiving side and they are on the giving side. It looks as if they, rather than God, are superior. My friend, we are not witnessing correctly for God—no matter how many people we buttonhole and tell about Jesus—unless you and I take the place where we are condemned and God is vindicated, and God is to be praised and honored. This is a tremendous lesson in this book.

> **I am as one mocked of his neighbor, who calleth upon God, and he answereth him: the just upright man is laughed to scorn.**
>
> **He that is ready to slip with his feet is as a lamp despised in the thought of him that is at ease [Job 12:4–5].**

Job is a very sick man, but he is standing up to these three men. He tells them, "You fellows are in a comfortable position and you are able to give advice to me, but I am slipping. I am falling, and you have no word for me at all."

For years I served as a pastor, and I realize now how a professional attitude enters into our lives. I would go the hospital to visit a sick

person, perhaps a dying person. I would pat him on the hand and say, "God will be with you," and I would pray for him and say, "God will lead you." Then I'd walk out. Well, the day came when I went to the hospital, not to visit someone, but to lie on that bed myself. When someone came to pray with me and walked out, I didn't walk out. I stayed there. My friend, I want to say to you, that is quite a different position to be in. Now I was in the other fellow's shoes. Now I was in bed and I was facing surgery. That is the time you need someone to help you and to comfort you. That is what Job is needing.

For the rest of the chapter, Job goes on to say that his friends do not have such superior wisdom. They are not the only ones who know about God. Job also knows about the power of God in the affairs of men.

Job now is bitter and sarcastic. His friends are not helping him at all, and he longs to appeal to God directly.

> **Lo, mine eye hath seen all this, mine ear hath heard and understood it.**

> **What ye know, the same do I know also: I am not inferior unto you [Job 13:1–2].**

He knows all the truths which his friends have expounded to him. They haven't told him anything new that he had not known before, and they have not helped him.

> **Surely I would speak to the Almighty, and I desire to reason with God [Job 13:3].**

Job would like to bypass his friends and appeal to God directly. He wants to reason with God. Oh, if only someone had been there to tell Job about the grace and the mercy of God and how God wanted to help him.

> **But ye are forgers of lies, ye are all physicians of no value [Job 13:4].**

He repeats that his friends have not been able to diagnose his case and that they are not helping him. They are like a doctor who has a patient with diabetes and says the cure would be to take out his lungs. They missed the whole point.

O that ye would altogether hold your peace! and it should be your wisdom [Job 13:5].

He tells them the best thing for them to do would be to keep quiet. He tells them that that would be smarter than what they were saying.

Hear now my reasoning, and hearken to the pleadings of my lips.

Will ye speak wickedly for God? and talk deceitfully for him? [Job 13:6–7].

He really speaks back to them. He says that when they are accusing him of committing some awful sin and that God is judging him, they are talking deceitfully for God. They are not representing God as they should. Job knows they are not God's direct representatives. They could have helped Job if they had brought him to the place where he could see himself as he really was. Instead, they put him on the defense. As a result, he is actually making a good case for himself. All of this makes it look bad for God. It looks as if God is to blame in all this.

Will ye accept his person? will ye contend for God?

Is it good that he should search you out? or as one man mocketh another, do ye so mock him?

He will surely reprove you, if ye do secretly accept persons [Job 13:8–10].

Job says that God is going to judge them for misrepresenting Him.

Shall not his excellency make you afraid? and his dread fall upon you?

Your remembrances are like unto ashes, your bodies to bodies of clay.

Hold your peace, let me alone, that I may speak, and let come on me what will.

Wherefore do I take my flesh in my teeth, and put my life in mine hand? [Job 13:11-14].

In the midst of all this, the faith of Job stands inviolate. He has experienced the onslaught of his friends who, by now, have actually become strangers to him, as we shall see.

Though he slay me, yet will I trust in him: but I will maintain mine own ways before him [Job 13:15].

This is Job's great statement of faith. Job's friends, you see, were accusing him of some gross secret sin such as immorality or dishonesty or some other sin of the flesh. Job is not guilty of anything like this. But here we begin to see the root of his problem. Job says that he will go into the presence of God and will defend himself there.

My friend, the minute you go into the presence of God to start defending yourself, you will lose your case. When you stand before Him, you can only plead guilty because He knows you. You can't go into the presence of God with an attorney who by some clever routine can clear you of the accusation. No attorney can annul God's statement that all have sinned and come short of the glory of God, that there is none righteous, no, not one, and that the soul that sinneth shall die. God just doesn't change that at all. No smart lawyer can get you out of that. Nor are you going to stand before some softhearted and softheaded judge. You are going to stand before the God of this universe who is the moral Ruler. No one can maintain a case before Him. The thing to do is to go in and plead guilty and cast yourself upon the mercy of the court. You will find that God has a mercy seat. It is a mercy seat because the blood of Jesus Christ is on it. Christ paid the price for your sin. My friend, that is the only way you can escape the penalty.

You can see that Job desperately needs someone to represent God to

him and keep him from trying to defend himself before Him. Someone needs to show him that he can cast himself on the mercy of God. This book has a tremendous message for us, as you can see.

He also shall be my salvation: for an hypocrite shall not come before him [Job 13:16].

There are glimmers of light that break through on this man's soul. He says, "He shall be my salvation." By the way, notice that it is the teaching of the Old Testament as well as the New Testament that God is our salvation. David held on to this fact, because David committed an awful sin. Of course he didn't *live* in sin, but he needed a Savior. He wrote, "He only is my rock and my salvation; he is my defence; I shall not be greatly moved" (Ps. 62:2). Salvation is not like a coin that you carry around in your pocket and might lose. Salvation is God. Today salvation is Jesus Christ. You either have Him or you don't trust Him. There are no other alternatives, friends. You stand on one side or the other. Either you are for Him or you are against Him. ". . . There is none other name under heaven given among men, whereby we must be saved" (Acts 4:12). He is the only "out" for the human family. It is marvelous that Job, who probably lived in the patriarchal age of the days of Abraham, Isaac, and Jacob, had a glimmer of light.

Hear diligently my speech, and my declaration with your ears [Job 13:17].

Job says, "Listen to me!"

Behold now, I have ordered my cause; I know that I shall be justified [Job 13:18].

Job thinks he has a good case even before God. He says that he knows he shall be justified, but he does not claim that on the grounds that Someone else obtained that justification for him.

There are people today who say, "Oh, I don't mind coming before God. I can stand on my good works." I have news for them: they have

already been condemned before God. My friend, we are *all* sinners. We live in a world that is in rebellion against God because our hearts are evil. Not one of us is so important that God needs us in His program here on earth. He could get along without us very nicely. But, thank God, He loves us and He made a way for us to be justified. The Judge had mercy on us and sent His own Son to pay our penalty. That is the reason He can justify us.

> **Who is he that will plead with me? for now, if I hold my tongue, I shall give up the ghost [Job 13:19].**

This is interesting. At the beginning Job said that he wanted to die. He wished he had never been born. Now he says that if he holds his tongue he shall give up the ghost. All right, Job, if you want to die, why don't you quit talking? You will notice he doesn't do that. He is going to talk. This is the way of little men—we all have a lot to say.

> **Only do not two things unto me: then will I not hide myself from thee.**

> **Withdraw thine hand far from me: and let not thy dread make me afraid [Job 13:20–21].**

Job is a frightened man.

> **Then call thou, and I will answer: or let me speak, and answer thou me [Job 13:22].**

He is telling God what to do. I'm afraid many of us do that. I hear so many people say they have unanswered prayers. No, there are no unanswered prayers. God always answers prayer, and many times He answers "no." At least He has said "no" to most of my prayers, but that *is* an answer.

We must admit that a lot of our praying is really giving orders to God. We pray as if we were top sergeants talking to a buck private in the rear ranks. We say, "You do that," or "You do it this way." But God doesn't move that way.

Job tries to tell God how He should handle his situation. But God says, "I am not moving according to your plan. I have a plan, and I am going to work it out in your life."

I had the privilege of speaking to a group of Christian college students at a state college, and I was rather amazed to hear some of these young people arguing about prayer. They said, "What's the use of praying? You can't change God." They felt there was no need for prayer. That reminded me of Job here. Their idea of prayer was that God should be the One who would come at their beck and call.

I tried to make it clear to them that the purpose of prayer is not to change God. Where did we ever get that idea? Do we think we can change God by prayer? God has already made His plan, and He has *all* the information. Neither can we tell Him anything in our prayer that He doesn't already know. The primary purpose of prayer is to change *us*. We often see a little motto—and I think it is partially true—that reads: "Prayer Changes Things." I think it does change things, but the important thing is that prayer changes us, my friend.

God is not a Western Union boy. Don't get the idea you just call Him to come and deliver a message for you or to you. That is what Job was trying to get Him to do here. I'm not pointing an accusing finger at Job, because I have done the very same thing.

> **How many are mine iniquities and sins? make me to know my transgression and my sin.**
>
> **Wherefore hidest thou thy face, and holdest me for thine enemy?**
>
> **Wilt thou break a leaf driven to and fro? and wilt thou pursue the dry stubble? [Job 13:23-25].**

Very candidly, Job is asking for a showdown with God. That is what he wants. He wants to know how many sins and iniquities he has so he will understand why he is being treated as he is. He says he is just like a leaf that has been driven to and fro and has been stepped on.

Thou puttest my feet also in the stocks, and lookest narrowly unto all my paths; thou settest a print upon the heels of my feet.

And he, as a rotten thing, consumeth, as a garment that is moth eaten [Job 13:27–28].

Job feels that he is just rotting away. He cannot see any point to his suffering at all.

JOB'S ELEGY ON DEATH

Man that is born of a woman is of few days, and full of trouble [Job 14:1].

There is nothing any truer than that; trouble is the common denominator of mankind. All of us have had trouble. As Eliphaz had said, "Yet man is born unto trouble, as the sparks fly upward" (Job 5:7). Trouble is a language that the whole human family knows.

He cometh forth like a flower, and is cut down: he fleeth also as a shadow, and continueth not [Job 14:2].

Job says that death is inevitable and that we must depart from this world. Life is like a shadow. When the sun goes down, what happens to the shadow? It is gone.

And dost thou open thine eyes upon such an one, and bringest me into judgment with thee? [Job 14:3].

Like a flower that has been cut down, or as a shadow that disappears, is my life. And yet God sees me and deals with me.

Who can bring a clean thing out of an unclean? not one [Job 14:4].

Then he goes on to state a great truth. We were all born sinners. David said, "Behold, I was shapen in iniquity and in sin did my mother conceive me" (Ps. 51:5). How could any of us be sinless creatures when we had a sinful father and a sinful mother? You cannot bring a clean thing out of an unclean. That is a universal rule.

> **Seeing his days are determined, the number of his months are with thee, thou hast appointed his bounds that he cannot pass [Job 14:5].**

Job says that as a human being he feels that he is pretty well hemmed in. David wrote, ". . . though I walk through the valley of the shadow of death . . ." (Ps. 23:4). Was he referrring to his death bed? No. From the very minute of birth when we start out in life we are walking through a canyon where the shadow of death is on us, and we keep going until it gets narrower and narrower and finally leads to death. We are always walking in the shadow of death! Someone has put it like this: "The moment that gives us life begins to take it away from us."

> **For there is hope of a tree, if it be cut down, that it will sprout again, and that the tender branch thereof will not cease.**
>
> **Though the root thereof was old in the earth, and the stock thereof die in the ground;**
>
> **Yet through the scent of water it will bud, and bring forth boughs like a plant.**
>
> **But man dieth, and wasteth away; yea, man giveth up the ghost, and where is he? [Job 14:7–10].**

A man may have made a tremendous success down here, been a famous person, and then he is gone. Where is he? There may be a few monuments around for him. Maybe a street or two are named after him. What good is that? What does that amount to?

Here is a breakthrough that reveals the faith of Job.

If a man die, shall he live again? all the days of my appointed time will I wait, till my change come.

Thou shalt call, and I will answer thee: thou wilt have a desire to the work of thine hands [Job 14:14–15].

It has always been a big question with man. "If a man die, shall he live again?" Even in death Job knows that God is going to call him, and he will answer that call. In other words, God is not through with us at our death. Death is not the end of it all. We will hear Job say again later on: ". . . I know that my redeemer liveth, and that he shall stand at the latter day upon the earth: And though after my skin worms destroy this body, yet in my flesh shall I see God: Whom I shall see for myself, and mine eyes shall behold, and not another; though my reins be consumed within me" (Job 19:25–27).

This entire chapter is a great elegy on death. I recommend that you read it in its entirety.

CHAPTER 15

THEME: Second discourse of Eliphaz

These men are pitting their minds one against another. Instead of seeing brawn pitted against brawn in athletic events, these folk liked to witness intellectual battles. We have completed one round of discourses. All three of the friends have spoken, and Job has answered each of them. Now we start on the second round of discourses. We could say this is the second inning if we were talking about baseball, or we could call it the second half if we were talking about basketball or football.

Remember that Eliphaz is the spiritualist. He has had a dream and a vision. He feels that he has had a remarkable experience and should be heard.

Many of the testimonies we hear in our day have little value because they rest truth on experience. First of all we should have *truth*, which is the Word of God; then experience should come out of that. Many experiences do not coincide with God's Word. I have heard testimonies given by so-called Christians who have had a "great experience" that is no more scriptural than the telephone directory.

Eliphaz bases his words on experience, and it is mighty hard to deal with a fellow like that.

Then answered Eliphaz the Temanite, and said,

Should a wise man utter vain knowledge, and fill his belly with the east wind?

Should he reason with unprofitable talk? or with speeches wherewith he can do no good? [Job 15:1–3].

My, they are really slugging it out with words in this intellectual foray. He says, "My goodness, Job, you certainly are windy. You're just doing empty talking." Again you can see that he is not helping Job. Actu-

ally, he is attacking Job to try to break him down and make him confess. That is not the way to treat a man in trouble like Job is.

> **Yea, thou castest off fear, and restrainest prayer before God.**
>
> **For thy mouth uttereth thine iniquity, and thou choosest the tongue of the crafty.**
>
> **Thine own mouth condemneth thee, and not I: yea, thine own lips testify against thee [Job 15:4–6].**

Eliphaz says that Job is his own accuser. He is really going after Job, as you can see.

> **Art thou the first man that was born? or wast thou made before the hills? [Job 15:7].**

You speak as if you know something, Job.

> **Hast thou heard the secret of God? and dost thou restrain wisdom to thyself?**
>
> **What knowest thou, that we know not? what understandest thou, which is not in us? [Job 15:8–9].**

Again he is arguing from a wrong premise.

He tries to put Job in a very bad light. He does not bring Job to the place where he can see that he is a man who has a great lack and a great need. There is no comfort for Job from his friend.

> **With us are both the gray-headed and very aged men, much elder than thy father [Job 15:10].**

Eliphaz defends himself and the two other friends by telling Job of their advantage of maturity over him. He says that wisdom is on their side and not on the side of Job. This is his argument here.

> **What is man, that he should be clean? and he which is
> born of a woman, that he should be righteous?
> [Job 15:14].**

It is true that all men are sinners, but Eliphaz and his friends say this
with the basic premise that Job has committed an awful, terrible sin
and that he ought to bring it out in the open and confess it.

> **Behold, he putteth no trust in his saints; yea, the heav-
> ens are not clean in his sight [Job 15:15].**

What he says about the heavens is also true. When the Lord Jesus
Christ died, He did not die only to redeem mankind; but in His plan of
redemption there is to be a new heaven and a new earth that will come
because He has redeemed us. It is a true statement that the heavens are
not clean in His sight.

> **How much more abominable and filthy is man, which
> drinketh iniquity like water? [Job 15:16].**

That is also a true statement. If the heavens are filthy and need redeeming, how much more does man need redeeming? Although it is true, it
is no more applicable to Job and his condition than it is to any other
human being.

> **The wicked man travaileth with pain all his days, and
> the number of years is hidden to the oppressor.**
>
> **A dreadful sound is in his ears; in prosperity the de-
> stroyer shall come upon him [Job 15:20–21].**

Here again is the suggestion that Job is wicked and is hiding something from them.

We must admit, however, that these men did not have a contemporary false psychology which says there is really nothing wrong with
man, that man has made a few mistakes, and his sin is really one of

ignorance, but it really is nothing that couldn't be cured by rubbing a little "salve" on it. These men had a truer concept than our modern men who teach that man is a superior creature because he is the product of evolution, and so is not responsible to a Creator. Although these men did not have the answer to the problem of Job, many of the things they said were absolutely true.

Eliphaz, instead of being a comforter, is a debater. He is not adding anything new but is playing the same old record over again. He has no new information since his first speech.

CHAPTERS 16 AND 17

THEME: Job's answer to Eliphaz

We will now hear Job answer Eliphaz for the second time. This is very much like a debate. First we hear one side, and then we hear from the other side. Actually it should not have been this way because these men had come to be Job's comforters. Instead of being comforters they have become debaters. They are really attempting to beat him down, attempting to gain an intellectual victory over him. But they are not winning the debate. My feeling is that it is a standoff. Eventually a young man who has been standing by enters in and picks up the argument. Finally, God will break in on the scene. That, of course, is what Job needs and what Job wants.

Eliphaz has just played the same old record over again. He is the dreamer. He has had a vision. He is a spiritualist. He claims to have some inside information that no one else has, but he didn't give any advance information after his first speech. He just comes up with the same old thing.

Then Job answered and said,

I have heard many such things: miserable comforters are ye all [Job 16:1–2].

Job says, "You haven't said anything new to me. You haven't said a thing that I haven't already heard. Besides, you are miserable comforters."

These men, I am confident, were friends of Job, but they ended up in a debate. Job has his chance to give a rebuttal after each man speaks, which is what we have here now.

Shall vain words have an end? or what emboldeneth thee that thou answerest? [Job 16:3].

Job is saying, "I would have thought you would have been ashamed to speak as you have. Those are vain words, empty words. They do not meet the need."

Unfortunately, a great many sermons are like that. Some of them are not even Bible-centered and cannot be used by the spirit of God. Unless the spirit of God can use a sermon, it will come to naught. It will be a vain, empty thing. There is a lot of preaching in the world today that is absolutely meaningless as far as worship of God and expounding His Word are concerned. The same can be said for a lot of the singing—and the entire service—in some of our churches. The fault may lie with the preacher, but it doesn't always rest there; sometimes the congregation, the listeners, can be responsible for the breakdown that takes place.

> **I also could speak as ye do: if your soul were in my soul's stead, I could heap up words against you, and shake mine head at you [Job 16:4].**

Job is telling them that if their situations were reversed, he could have given a little speech of condemnation against them.

Paul was concerned about this type of thing, and he wrote to believers in order to counteract it, "Brethren, if a man be overtaken in a fault, ye which are spiritual, restore such an one in the spirit of meekness; considering thyself, lest thou also be tempted" (Gal. 6:1). Don't go to debate with such a person. Don't go to preach to him. Restore him in the spirit of meekness, which was illustrated by our Lord when he washed the feet of those who were His own. He is still doing that today. When you and I confess our sins, ". . . he is faithful and just to forgive us our sins, and to cleanse us from all unrighteousness" (1 John 1:9). He still washes feet; that is, He still cleanses his own. But He also set us an example. If you are going to wash someone's feet, you can't put yourself above him, look down upon him, point your finger, and begin to preach at him. You will need to kneel down and take the place of a servant to wash feet. That is quite a bit different from arguing with the person.

It's too bad that these friends didn't come to Job in that way, but

they didn't. They came preaching at him. Realizing that, he tells them
that if he were in their position, he could do the same thing. He could
shake his head at them and heap up words against them.

> But I would strengthen you with my mouth, and the
> moving of my lips should assuage your grief [Job 16:5].

Job says that he would approach them in a different way. He says he
would want to strengthen them. He would want to comfort them. He
would want to "wash their feet," that is, restore them to fellowship—
which is what they should have done for him.

> Though I speak, my grief is not assuaged: and though I
> forbear, what am I eased? [Job 16:6].

Job is not helped at all.

> But now he hath made me weary: thou hast made deso-
> late all my company.
> And thou hast filled me with wrinkles, which is a wit-
> ness against me: and my leanness rising up in me
> beareth witness to my face [Job 16:7–8].

Job says, "You've made an old man out of me—you have filled me with
wrinkles."

> He teareth me in his wrath, who hateth me: he gnasheth
> upon me with his teeth; mine enemy sharpeneth his
> eyes upon me.
> They have gaped upon me with their mouth; they have
> smitten me upon the cheek reproachfully; they have
> gathered themselves together against me.
> God hath delivered me to the ungodly, and turned me
> over into the hands of the wicked [Job 16:9–11].

These men are the same as the ungodly. They are supposed to be friends to Job, but they treated him like an enemy. And do you know that there are Christians today who can be meaner to you than many of the unsaved people? There is nothing meaner than a Christian when he is mean. So Job classifies his friends as ungodly. You see, they think they are defending God, but in doing so they are unfair and even brutal in their accusations against Job.

> **I was at ease, but he hath broken me asunder: he hath also taken me by my neck, and shaken me to pieces, and set me up for his mark [Job 16:12].**

Job recognizes that God has permitted this to happen to him. Many times when I was a boy and would go hunting, I would see the dog catch a rabbit. He would grab the rabbit by the nape of the neck and shake it—oh, how he would shake it! Apparently Job had seen that too. Job said that that was how God was shaking him. God does that sometimes, friends.

> **His archers compass me round about, he cleaveth my reins asunder, and doth not spare; he poureth out my gall upon the ground [Job 16:13].**

Thinking of the bitterness of gall, he is saying that his bitterness is poured out of him.

> **He breaketh me with breach upon breach, he runneth upon me like a giant [Job 16:14].**

He says that God has been walking up and down on him like a giant. Job feels that God has made a door mat out of him, as it were. You couldn't find any more vivid description than Job gives us here.

Great writers of the past, novelists, poets, and essayists, have read and reread the Book of Job. Its language is superb. Its descriptions are magnificent. I would recommend it to you for your reading so that it becomes a part of you. The beauty of the language here is wonderful.

> **I have sewed sackcloth upon my skin, and defiled my horn in the dust.**
>
> **My face is foul with weeping, and on my eyelids is the shadow of death [Job 16:15–16].**

Have you noticed how close to death Job was? He wished for it, and yet he avoided it. He stood right on the threshold of death during all of this time. I think he felt that at any moment he might die. He was a sick man, a very sick man.

> **Not for any injustice in mine hands: also my prayer is pure [Job 16:17].**

Now again we see emerging the thing in the heart and life of Job that needed to be dealt with. You see, his friends have not been leading him to a place where he would judge himself. Instead, they actually ministered to a spirit of self-vindication. They put him on the defensive. The minute Job started to defend himself, he put God at a disadvantage. Job justified himself instead of justifying God. The problem was that his friends condemned Job instead of leading Job to condemn himself. They were using the wrong approach with him.

The minute a person begins to defend himself, he puts himself in the position which John very candidly stated. "If we say that we have no sin, we deceive ourselves, and the truth is not in us . . . If we say that we have not sinned, we make him a liar, and his word is not in us" (1 John 1:8, 10). That makes God a liar. It puts God in the place of being blamed. It takes God from the position of being the Judge and puts Him down as the One who is judged, the guilty one, the criminal. A person then is bringing a charge against God.

There are actually many people who sit in judgment upon God. That is what Job is actually doing here. He is justifying himself by saying, "Not for any injustice in mine hands"—the minute he says that, he is also saying that God is wrong in letting this happen to him.

Job says, "Also, my prayer is pure." I have heard that same statement coming from Christians. Friend, I doubt whether any of us pray a

pure prayer. That is the reason I always tell the Lord, "I am asking this in Jesus' name"—because I know that Vernon McGee would not get through on his own. Job thinks *he* would get through.

O earth, cover not thou my blood, and let my cry have no place [Job 16:18].

Now Job cried out in spectacular language. He asks the earth not to cover up his blood. If the blood of Abel cried out to God, then certainly Job thinks his blood ought to cry out to God.

Friend, God does not cover up blood. And God sees the blood that Christ shed, especially when you reject it.

Also now, behold, my witness is in heaven, and my record is on high [Job 16:19].

The Bible all the way through teaches that God keeps a record of us. There are those today who like to pooh-pooh such an idea. They say, "Can you imagine God up there sitting at a desk keeping books?" Friend, who said he is keeping books? God doesn't need to do that. If a mere man can make a little machine called a computer, don't you think God can have a way of keeping records that surpasses anything we can imagine? I am of the opinion that everything we have ever said, everything we have ever done, is recorded. I don't know about you, but I can say for myself that I don't ever want to see the record that is made of me. I am very happy that some of it is blotted out under the blood of Jesus Christ. Oh, thank God for that!

My friends scorn me: but mine eye poureth out tears unto God [Job 16:20].

This is the picture of Job as he sits there in that desolate place with tears streaming from his eyes. His friends stand around him and look at him in scorn and call him a hypocrite and accuse him of being a liar. They don't know him, they don't know God, and they don't know themselves.

O that one might plead for a man with God, as a man pleadeth for his neighbour! [Job 16:21].

Here is another of those cries of Job. How wonderful it is for believers to know that we have an Intercessor. We have an Advocate. We have an Attorney who represents us before God. Everything has been taken care of for us. We have One who pleads for us before God. "For there is one God, and one mediator between God and men, the man Christ Jesus" (1 Tim. 2:5). Friend, He would like to be your Advocate if He isn't already.

My breath is corrupt, my days are extinct, the graves are ready for me [Job 17:1].

Job knew about halitosis—bad breath—and he didn't have the mouthwashes we have today! What it really means is that he is very sick. The grave is ready for him. It is as if he were saying that he has one foot in the grave and the other on a banana peel. He thinks he is dying.

Are there not mockers with me? and doth not mine eye continue in their provocation? [Job 17:2].

Here Job is dying, and his friends stand around and mock him. What a picture this is! These men who had come to comfort him are actually debating with him and condemning him. My friend, it is possible to be a hard-boiled Christian and not be very helpful to the poor sinners in this world.

We need to recognize that there are times for harsh words. God will be very harsh with Job, but He also is going to comfort him. God is going to help him and God is going to restore him. Oh, that you and I might see that God is a God of judgment, but that He is also the God of mercy and the God of grace.

Lay down now, put me in a surety with thee; who is he that will strike hands with me? [Job 17:3].

Job says that at least they could shake hands with him.

> **For thou hast hid their heart from understanding: there-fore shalt thou not exalt them.**
>
> **He that speaketh flattery to his friends, even the eyes of his children shall fail [Job 17:4–5].**

And he pleads that he does not want to be flattered. He doesn't want them to "butter him up." He continues in this vein and then concludes that he is on his deathbed.

> **If I wait, the grave is mine house: I have made my bed in the darkness [Job 17:13].**

He never expects to leave that dump heap outside the city—he thinks it is his deathbed.

> **I have said to corruption, Thou art my father: to the worm, Thou art my mother, and my sister.**
>
> **And where is now my hope? as for my hope, who shall see it?**
>
> **They shall go down to the bars of the pit, when our rest together is in the dust [Job 17:14–16].**

He says that corruption and decay are closer to him than his father or mother. His parents had brought him into the world, but now he is closer to death than he is to them. His body, which is so weary and so sick, is ready to return to the dust.

CHAPTER 18

THEME: The second discourse of Bildad

This is now the second round for Bildad, the Shuhite. This is his rebuttal. The interesting thing is that he really hasn't anything new to contribute at all. You will recall that he is a traditionalist. He has a lot of old sayings and proverbs that he strings along like a string of beads. He will do that again here. He has a whole series of epigrams and pious platitudes and slick clichés. Some of them are good, but none of them throw light on Job's case.

Then answered Bildad the Shuhite, and said,

How long will it be ere ye make an end of words? mark, and afterwards we will speak.

Wherefore are we counted as beasts, and reputed vile in your sight? [Job 18:1–3].

To state it very bluntly Bildad is saying, "Job, if you would shut up, then we could speak. You should quit talking and start listening. You have been doing the talking when you should have been listening to us." Actually, all of them, Job and his friends, could have refrained from talking and been listening. But they were not prepared for the voice of God at this time. God is preparing Job to hear His voice, and later he will listen.

Bildad asks Job why he holds them in such contempt and why they are vile in his sight. The answer is obvious. This is the way they have been looking at Job. That is why I say that at this point it is a stand-off between Job and his friends. I think they have been glaring at each other during this debate. These men who had come to him as his friends are no longer his friends.

He teareth himself in his anger: shall the earth be forsaken for thee? and shall the rock be removed out of his place? [Job 18:4].

Bildad is asking, "Do you think God is going to run His universe just to suit you?" Bildad, you remember, is a traditionalist, and he rests everything on the past. He feels that anything that was true in the past is also good enough for today. That is the method which he uses.

"Job, can you not show some sense so that we may come to an understanding here? Do you think that your contempt for us as incompetent and your rage at divine dealings with you are going to release you now from the trap you are in?"

Yea, the light of the wicked shall be put out, and the spark of his fire shall not shine [Job 18:5].

Nothing truer could be spoken, but it does not apply to Job.

The light shall be dark in his tabernacle, and his candle shall be put out with him.

The steps of his strength shall be straitened, and his own counsel shall cast him down.

For he is cast into a net by his own feet, and he walketh upon a snare [Job 18:6–8].

"Job, you have been caught in a net like a fish, and it is not because we have done anything. We are supposed to be here to help you, and you don't listen to us. You are in that position because there is some secret sin in your life. You have walked into a trap."

The gin shall take him by the heel, and the robber shall prevail against him.

The snare is laid for him in the ground, and a trap for him in the way [Job 18:9–10].

The *gin* means a trap. "A trap will take you. You have been caught like a bear in a trap because you have been fooling around with the bait. If that weren't true, you wouldn't have been caught."

You can see that Bildad gives these little pious platitudes and works them like a geometry problem. First you take all the steps of the proof, then you come to the conclusion, and that's it. However, life is not quite like that. For one thing, it is easy in life to begin with some wrong premises. If the premises are accurate, one can come up with a good deduction. But if the premises are wrong, the conclusion will also be wrong. If A equals ten and you make it equal fifteen, you will not arrive at the correct answer to your problem—even if you use the right methods.

These men are all trying to put down their formulas, but they are putting the wrong premises into their formulas. Bildad comes up with a hard and fast rule which states that Job has walked into a trap, that it has been his own doing, and that it could not be otherwise. Another translation would be, "For he is sent into the net by his own feet and he walketh on the meshes."

> **Terrors shall make him afraid on every side, and shall drive him to his feet.**
>
> **His strength shall be hunger-bitten, and destruction shall be ready at his side.**
>
> **It shall devour the strength of his skin: even the first-born of death shall devour his strength.**
>
> **His confidence shall be rooted out of his tabernacle, and it shall bring him to the king of terrors.**
>
> **It shall dwell in his tabernacle, because it is none of his: brimstone shall be scattered upon his habitation.**
>
> **His roots shall be dried up beneath, and above shall his branch be cut off.**
>
> **His remembrance shall perish from the earth, and he shall have no name in the street [Job 18:11–17].**

He is saying that disease shall waste the body of the wicked. The fire of God will destroy his habitation, and his name shall be blotted out. His family shall perish—he will have neither son nor grandson. His desolation shall astonish future generations. All of this is true of the wicked, but it is not applicable to Job. A statement can be absolutely true, and yet have no application to an individual situation.

This is the reason, I feel, that a great deal of so-called "counseling" today is dangerous. I think there are many fine Christian psychologists; I know some of them, and I would recommend them. But, candidly, many psychologists often have premises which are not accurate, and for that reason they are not able to counsel.

These men are trying to counsel Job, but they are not able to do so. Bildad says the wicked are going to be judged. The wicked will be blotted out. That is true. Look in our own day to the fate of Hitler and Stalin and other dictators. As they lived, they died. Although his statement is true, Job is not that kind of man by any means.

> **He shall be driven from light into darkness, and chased out of the world [Job 18:18].**

That is a figurative expression of the wicked, but it does not apply to Job.

> **He shall neither have son nor nephew among his people, nor any remaining in his dwellings.**

> **They that come after him shall be astonished at his day, as they that went before were affrighted [Job 18:19–20].**

Any man likes to have sons and daughters and grandchildren. They are a source of pride and satisfaction. Sometimes the wicked have more offspring than anyone else. Job, at this time, does not have one child left to him. They have all been slain. It is actually cruel for Bildad to talk in this way to Job. We shall see later on that God is going to make it up to Job and give him more children.

Surely such are the dwellings of the wicked, and this is the place of him that knoweth not God [Job 18:21].

So we see that Bildad gives a description of the wicked. He shows the position of the wicked and the end of the wicked. He classes Job with the wicked and tells him that he is at the end of the road. He says, "This is the way it is, Job, and the description fits you." Of course, if one looks at the circumstances, one must admit that it looks as if Job does fit this description. These friends simply could not believe that what had happened to Job could have happened for some other reason. They believe that he is wicked and that he is hiding some secret sin, and they will not accept any other reason for his suffering.

When Job answers them, he is going to say, "Can't you conceive it possible that God has entangled me in His net and left His action unexplained? There must be an explanation for it, but your explanation may not be right."

CHAPTER 19

THEME: Job's answer to Bildad

As you can see, the mistake Job is beginning to make is this: he knows they are wrong, but their being wrong does not make him right. His attitude is wrong also. He has a wrong conception of God at this time, although light breaks in from time to time.

> **Then Job answered and said,**
>
> **How long will ye vex my soul, and break me in pieces with words? [Job 19:1–2].**

If this had been a physical combat like a football game, the coach would have said, "The opposition tore down our defense." Job's so-called friends have been breaking down his defense.

> **These ten times have ye reproached me: ye are not ashamed that ye make yourselves strange to me [Job 19:3].**

The more they talked, the more alienated from Job they became. They were not right, but neither was Job. Job thought that because they were wrong, he would be right. If Job's conscience and his life had been open in the presence of God, what position should he have taken? Let me make a suggestion: I think that he should not have replied to his friends at all. Unfortunately, most of us think we must defend ourselves.

I thank God for giving me the gift of preaching and teaching, but I will be very frank with you and say that it is a dangerous gift to have because it puts you up where you can be shot at and where you can be criticized. People have asked me from time to time, "Why don't you defend yourself? Why don't you write a little book to defend yourself?"

The answer is that I don't need to. As someone has stated it, your friends who know you don't need an explanation, and your enemies wouldn't believe you anyway.

I have learned that in time things pretty much answer themselves. I don't think a person needs to defend himself in these cases. My suggestion would be that Job should not have answered these friends at all. He should have simply bowed in sweet submission. I think he should have listened to what they had to say, then told them good-bye and shown them the front gate of the city. But Job was determined to vindicate himself.

I can think of some men whom time has vindicated. William Booth, the founder of the Salvation Army, was accused very cruelly. He sought to defend himself, but he needn't have done so. Time has shown the truth of the matter. The later Dr. M. R. DeHann was severely attacked when he was pastor of a church. There were those who sought to defend him, but he really didn't need any defense. Time has justified his actions and revealed the fact that those charges made against him were false indeed.

I personally think that Job should have taken the position of silence and that he should not have come out with this defense of himself. He has become alienated from them. If he had kept silent, he would not have had ten reproaches from them. Apparently he doesn't see that.

And be it indeed that I have erred, mine error remaineth with myself [Job 19:4].

"No one knows any error in me but myself." His friends are not able to point it out, and the implication is that he isn't aware of any error himself. Someone has said that the Lord did not make us perfect, but He made us blind to our errors. Although I don't think the Lord is responsible for that, I think the statement is probably true. We are not perfect, but most of us are blind to our faults. Job is a man who is blind to a great many of his faults.

If indeed ye will magnify yourselves against me, and plead against me my reproach:

> **Know now that God hath overthrown me, and hath com-passed me with his net [Job 19:5–6].**

Bildad has said that Job had walked into a net, but Job maintains that God has done this and that God hasn't given an explanation for it. Couldn't it be that God has done this for some reason that He has not explained to Job? Of course, but the friends are determined that their explanation is the right one.

Now he pleads with his friends.

> **Behold, I cry out of wrong, but I am not heard: I cry aloud, but there is no judgment.**
>
> **He hath fenced up my way that I cannot pass, and he hath set darkness in my paths.**
>
> **He hath stripped me of my glory, and taken the crown from my head.**
>
> **He hath destroyed me on every side, and I am gone: and mine hope hath he removed like a tree.**
>
> **He hath also kindled his wrath against me, and he counteth me unto him as one of his enemies [Job 19:7–11].**

He says that God is treating him very harshly and that there must be an explanation for it. The purpose of God must be different from the explanation that his friends give to him, but Job confesses he doesn't know what that purpose is.

He goes on to tell how his brethren have forsaken him, his acquaintances are estranged from him, his friends have forgotten him, the maids that live in his house count him as a stranger, his servants will not answer his call, and his wife is a stranger to him. Even the young children have despised him. He is so thin that his bone cleaves to his skin, and he says, ". . . I am escaped with the skin of my teeth" (Job 19:20). He asks his friends for their pity.

**Oh that my words were now written! oh that they were
printed in a book!**

**That they were graven with an iron pen and lead in the
rock for ever! [Job 19:23-24].**

Job wishes that his words were written out and put in a book. He
would be willing for his worst enemy to write them. He would like
them engraven in the rock so he could say, "Look, this is what my
enemy says about me, and he has to praise me."

Would you want your worst enemy to write your biography? I'm not
sure that I'd want even my best friend to write mine. I am satisfied to
let my biography stand on God's books where it will be accurate,
which is the important thing.

Now Job will express his great faith. His friends have been attempting to break him down, which is actually the Devil's subtle attempt.
The Devil, through his friends, has been able to bring Job to the place
where he is not humble but is still trying to vindicate himself before
God. However, Job has not hit rock bottom yet. These friends have not
broken him down completely. He has a living, real faith in God, and
here he utters one of the great statements in the Bible. It is not only that
the statement is great, but it is great because the man who said it is a
sick man who is ready to expire. He has lost everything; he is under
the discipline of Almighty God, and he feels the lash upon his back.
Still he is able to say:

**For I know that my redeemer liveth, and that he shall
stand at the latter day upon the earth:**

**And though after my skin worms destroy this body, yet
in my flesh shall I see God:**

**Whom I shall see for myself, and mine eyes shall be-
hold, and not another; though my reins be consumed
within me [Job 19:25-27].**

When Job became ill and was in the shock of all his troubles, he said he
wanted to die. He was not speaking of annihilation. He was speaking

of the death which would get him away from his troubles. I think that
is obvious. He knew he would be raised again. He knew that in his
flesh he would see God. He knew that even if the worms destroyed his
body after death, yet in his flesh he would see God. He believed in the
resurrection of the dead.

Friends, these bodies of ours are going to return to the dust. The
bodies of the dead in Christ will be put to sleep, but the spirit will go
to be with Christ immediately. How wonderful this is!

Job again cries out to his friends, having made this great statement.

> **But ye should say, Why persecute we him, seeing the
> root of the matter is found in me?**
>
> **Be ye afraid of the sword: for wrath bringeth the pun-
> ishments of the sword, that ye may know there is a judg-
> ment [Job 19:28–29].**

"Don't you fear the judgment of God for the things you have been saying to Me?" In spite of all their accusations, Job has kept his faith. He
believes the Redeemer is coming and that he himself is numbered with
the redeemed.

CHAPTER 20

Zophar is the last man to speak in this round. We are in the second round of the debate, and Zophar is the third man in this round. We find that there will be a third round and that it is going to be a brief one. Zophar won't even get in on the third round. It will simply end in a standoff before Zophar has another chance to speak.

Remember that Zophar is the legalist. He believes that God works according to law and order. That is true, of course, but that throne of law and order in judgment has become a throne of grace. Zophar knew nothing about that.

I suppose today we would say that Zophar has the scientific mind. He thinks you pour life into the test tube and it will always come out a certain way. He is the one who says that things can never be changed, that all things continue as they have from the foundation of the world. He knows nothing of the grace of God.

He comes on strong. He is actually less impressive this time around than he was before, although he is more brutal and cruel than he was before. He is a hard slugger. He hits Job hard because he realizes this may be his last time around. Although he introduces nothing new, he pours out all that he has to pour out. He rests upon his seniority, and he resorts to the same legalism. He holds to the theory that Job is a very wicked person because of the law that the wicked must be punished. That will be his emphasis here.

> **Then answered Zophar the Naamathite, and said,**
>
> **Therefore do my thoughts cause me to answer, and for this I make haste.**
>
> **I have heard the check of my reproach, and the spirit of my understanding causeth me to answer [Job 20:1–3].**

He sounds like a politician running for office. He says he is capable of answering. I never heard of a man running for office who didn't say he

was more qualified than his opponent; he doesn't mind telling you that. When a man says that, he does lack modesty! Now this man Zophar comes on like a politician. He is going to present his case with the same type of an argument which he had used before. He says that he is going to repeat an age-established fact. Well, what is it?

> **Knowest thou not this of old, since man was placed upon earth [Job 20:4].**

Here it is. Here is his specific conclusion, which he poured into the test tube of the past and found to be true.

> **Though his excellency mount up to the heavens, and his head reach unto the clouds;**

> **Yet he shall perish for ever like his own dung: they which have seen him shall say, Where is he? [Job 20:6–7].**

He can get dramatic, too. "Though his excellency mount up to the heavens, and his head reach unto the clouds." The language is tremendous in this book. As I have said, people will read the Book of Job for its expressive language, even though they may not read any other book in the Bible.

Eventually the wicked perish. Some of our contemporary young people hear about Hitler and they do not simply say, "Where is he?" but they even ask, "Who was he?" They don't even recall him. I remember that when I was a little boy, people spoke of Kaiser Wilhelm as though he were the Devil incarnate. He is gone. All of them are gone. They had a long moment, but now they are gone.

> **He shall fly away as a dream, and shall not be found: yea, he shall be chased away as a vision of the night.**

> **The eye also which saw him shall see him no more; neither shall his place any more behold him.**

> **His children shall seek to please the poor, and his hands shall restore their goods [Job 20:8–10].**

Very candidly, it seems to me that man is the greatest failure in God's universe. Consider the brevity of man. They tell us how old the rocks are—even the rocks that came from the moon. Man hasn't been around that long; he is a Johnny-come-lately in the universe. Friends, if there is not an eternity ahead of us, man is the most colossal failure that God has ever made. His life is brief. He flies away as a dream.

Dr. Bill Anderson, a great preacher in Dallas, Texas, was a tremendous inspiration to me when I was a student. He met one of his deacons on the street and somewhat surprised him with this unusual question: "Suppose when we get to heaven into the presence of God, we find that the Christian life wasn't essential to our getting there. What would be your viewpoint?" This deacon looked him straight in the eye and said, "If we get to heaven and find that all this business of the Christian life was nothing in the world but our own imagination, I'm going to say to the Lord that it was very much worthwhile. It was worth it all."

Now while I believe that is true—that the Christian life is worth it all for the here and now—even then there is a little tug of disappointment at our hearts if that is all there is. Why? Because we want eternity. God has set eternity in our hearts because it is *there*, and man is going to move on into eternity.

Zophar is calling Job not only wicked, but a hypocrite. His whole speech describes the fall of a wicked man. He says such a man may attain eminence, but that just simply means that his fall is going to be greater. His implication is that that is what has happened to Job.

> **His bones are full of the sin of his youth, which shall lie down with him in the dust.**

> **He hath swallowed down riches, and he shall vomit them up again: God shall cast them out of his belly.**

> **Because he hath oppressed and hath forsaken the poor; because he hath violently taken away an house which he builded not;**

> **Because he hath oppressed and hath forsaken the poor; because he hath violently taken away an house which he builded not;**

Surely he shall not feel quietness in his belly, he shall
not save of that which he desired.

There shall none of his meat be left; therefore shall no
man look for his goods [Job 20:11, 15, 19–21].

He suggests that such a man is like fuel which will be consumed. He
is like an evil vision which will disappear. His evil is like a sweet
morsel that he keeps under his tongue, but it will turn to gall within
him. It is like food that he eats, but God will compel him to disgorge
his unjustly amassed fortune and will force him to make restitution to
his victims.

When he is about to fill his belly, God shall cast the fury
of his wrath upon him, and shall rain it upon him while
he is eating. [Job 20:23].

Although nothing could escape his greed, he will be reduced to poverty. Worst of all, God shall cast the fury of his wrath upon him.

All darkness shall be hid in his secret places: a fire not
blown shall consume him; it shall go ill with him that is
left in his tabernacle.

The heaven shall reveal his iniquity; and the earth shall
rise up against him.

The increase of his house shall depart, and his goods
shall flow away in the day of his wrath [Job 20:26–28].

"A fire not blown shall consume him." In other words, he will become
a raging flame, and all his prosperity will go up in flames—there will
be no avenue of escape.

He sums it by saying,

This is the portion of a wicked man from God, and the
heritage appointed unto him by God [Job 20:29].

His implication, of course, is that the "wicked man" is Job. That is a
pretty bitter dose for a man in Job's condition, but Job is ready to answer him. He is going to defend himself, and he comes on strong, as
we shall see.

CHAPTER 21

THEME: Job's sixth answer

Job is still able to come back with an answer. I think it would have been better if he had not tried to answer Zophar's brutal accusation, but he is going to defend himself again.

He tells them that he is growing weary of their false charges. He appeals his case to a higher court. He agrees with them that the wicked will be punished but insists that this does not apply to his case.

> But Job answered and said,
>
> Hear diligently my speech, and let this be your consolations.
>
> Suffer me that I may speak; and after that I have spoken, mock on [Job 21:1–3].

Job wants their attention and sarcastically says that he is going to console them.

> As for me, is my complaint to man? and if it were so, why should not my spirit be troubled? [Job 21:4].

He is not taking his complaint to men; he is appealing to God.

> Mark me, and be astonished, and lay your hand upon your mouth [Job 21:5].

In other words, "Shut up!"

> Wherefore do the wicked live, become old, yea, are mighty in power?
>
> Their seed is established in their sight with them, and their offspring before their eyes.

Their houses are safe from fear, neither is the rod of God upon them.

Their bull gendereth, and faileth not; their cow calveth, and casteth not her calf [Job 21:7–10].

Job is now going to point out a fallacy in their argument. The wicked do not always suffer in this life; in fact, they may prosper. They are not always cut off; sometimes they attain old age, their property remains intact, and their children are able to inherit it.

They send forth their little ones like a flock, and their children dance.

They take the timbrel and harp, and rejoice at the sound of the organ.

They spend their days in wealth, and in a moment go down to the grave [Job 21:11–13].

They may have a whole flock of children. They dance and are gay and rejoice. They have a good time, and they live it up. You may say that their fall is going to be apparent, but you are mistaken. Like others, they go down to the grave but without catastrophe striking them before hand.

Job had been a rancher, and he points out that some of the wicked people are very prosperous cattlemen with big, prosperous families. I can remember when I was a boy in West Texas that some of the biggest drunkards in the neighborhood were also the biggest ranchers in the area. Where are they today? They are gone. Their sons apparently are following right in their footsteps, and they are going to disappear also. But they *do* prosper. Job calls attention to that.

You will remember that this was also an observation of David. He said, "I have seen the wicked in great power, and spreading himself like a green bay tree" (Ps. 37:35). However, David found, too, that God finally moves in judgment against the wicked.

We can look around in our own country today. We know certain family names that stand for money, and they have no reputation for

godliness. We find them in politics and in high society. They don't seem to suffer as other people suffer. Maybe sometimes this causes you to wonder. It is as Job is saying here, the wicked do prosper.

> **Therefore they say unto God, Depart from us; for we desire not the knowledge of thy ways.**
>
> **What is the Almighty, that we should serve him? and what profit should we have, if we pray unto him? [Job 21:14–15].**

They are godless. They don't want God. They insultingly say that they don't need God nor desire to know His ways. What could God give to them that they can't get for themselves?

> **Lo, their good is not in their hand: the counsel of the wicked is far from me [Job 21:16].**

Job is saying, "I don't belong in that class. I am not one of the wicked. What you lay down as an inevitable truth does not always work out to be true. Besides, even if it were true, it does not apply to me!"

> **How oft is the candle of the wicked put out! and how oft cometh their destruction upon them! God distributeth sorrows in his anger [Job 21:17].**

Those exclamation marks should probably be question marks—but either way, he is saying that the wicked have no more problems than the average person has.

> **They are as stubble before the wind, and as chaff that the storm carrieth away.**
>
> **God layeth up his iniquity for his children: he rewardeth him, and he shall know it.**
>
> **His eyes shall see his destruction, and he shall drink of the wrath of the Almighty [Job 21:18–20].**

However, death is no respector of persons, and the time comes when death knocks at the door of the wicked. There comes a time of judgment when "he shall drink of the wrath of the Almighty." So Job shows his friends that their proverbs are not always true, but that doesn't mean that God is not going to judge the wicked someday.

One time I heard a friend of mine say to a man who was apologizing for being drunk, "Don't apologize. You go ahead and drink it up now, boy, because in this life is the only place you can get it. Where you are going, they don't serve it. I don't blame you for getting all you can here." The wicked might as well enjoy every pleasure available to them because this is their last chance. The wicked are going to be judged eventually.

Job is confident that God will judge the wicked—there is no question about that.

> **Have ye not asked them that go by the way? and do ye not know their tokens,**
>
> **That the wicked is reserved to the day of destruction? they shall be brought forth to the day of wrath [Job 21:29–30].**

The judgment of the wicked may not be until the Great White Throne Judgment, but judgment will come eventually. God will permit the sinner to live it up down here if that's what he wants to do. You see, God is gracious. God is long-suffering. The goodness and the forebearance and the long-suffering of God should lead us to repentance.

I know that today we look at the rich who are enjoying life. The jet set goes from the United States to Europe and to Mexico from resort to resort. My, they really live it up, and God permits them to do it. But remember this: "The wicked is reserved to the day of destruction." We don't hear much said about that in these days.

This is the answer of Job to Zophar. May I say that it is a good answer. But we see that Job is still justifying himself. There is no thought of repentance in this speech by Job.

CHAPTER 22

THEME: The third discourse of Eliphaz

Here we come to the third inning, if you please. This is the third time that these men get into the arena to battle an intellectual battle. This kind of thing is not so attractive today. We had debate teams and that type of contest when I was going to college, but it was no more popular then than it is now.

Today we build bigger and better stadiums all over this country. It is a mighty poor city that doesn't have a gleaming, multi-million dollar stadium for athletic events. However, very little money goes for the intellectual and even less for the spiritual exercise. Here in Job it is an intellectual battle and a spiritual battle. You know, very few of us have ever been out on the football field carrying the ball or charging or blocking. Very few of us have ever gone up to bat in a major league, but all of us are out in the arena of life in a spiritual battle. This does not seem important to most people. They would rather go and sit in the bleachers and watch somebody else carry the ball. Well, my friend, you and I are fighting a spiritual battle. Paul tells us that we are wrestling and that the wrestling match is going on right now.

This kind of intellectual and spiritual battle excited the people in that day. We think they were uncivilized then. We are the ones who build the multi-million dollar stadiums for physical combat and fail to emphasize the intellectual combat.

You will remember that Eliphaz is the man who had the remarkable experience. He had a strange and mysterious vision. He is a spiritualist. He is the one who says, "I have seen."

Then Eliphaz the Temanite answered and said,

Can a man be profitable unto God, as he that is wise may be profitable unto himself? [Job 22:1–2].

The very nature of the question reveals that a man cannot be profitable to God. He is asking, "Job, you sure think a lot of yourself, but what do

you suppose God thinks of you?" He thinks Job is acting as if God might derive some benefit from his behavior and that if God were not restraining him, he might become too strong for God—that God is holding Job back for this reason. Well, Eliphaz is certainly off target. And it is certainly not comforting to a man who at this moment does need help and light from heaven.

Eliphaz' question applies to some church members I have known who think they are profitable to God. Some folk seem to think they make a real contribution to God down here and that He is rather fortunate to have them on His team. They seem to think that when they get to heaven, heaven will really be improved because of who they are. We need to recognize that man is not profitable to God. We are all unprofitable, which means we are like a bunch of spoiled fruit. Jesus told a parable about service and He concluded, "So likewise ye, when ye shall have done all those things which are commanded you, say, We are unprofitable servants: we have done that which was our duty to do" (Luke 17:10).

> **Is it any pleasure to the Almighty, that thou art righteous? or is it gain to him, that thou makest thy ways perfect? [Job 22:3]**

These men do sense a little chink in the armor of this man Job. It will be glaring and apparent in just a few chapters. The trouble is that they do not really make a correct diagnosis of the man, and they certainly do not know the remedy. They are not able to comfort him and bring him help as they should. The fact that Job claims to be a righteous man doesn't cause God to jump up and down with glee and throw His hat in the air.

I have a feeling that there are a great many professing Christians who rest so much upon themselves and who they are that they really are not trusting Christ. Let me emphasize that we bring no pleasure to the Almighty because we have been good little Sunday School boys and have pins for perfect attendance. A great many folk think that the Lord is delighted with that sort of thing. I don't think so. We need to recognize who we are, and we need to recognize our utter dependence

upon God—our great need of Him. We are to be looking to Him instead of trying to impress Him with who we are and what we are doing.

> **Will he reprove thee for fear of thee? will he enter with thee into judgment? [Job 22:4].**

Eliphaz asks Job, "Are you so righteous and so perfect that God has to be afraid to deal with you?" We need to understand that when God says Job was "perfect" it means he stood in a right relationship with God through sacrifice–we know he offered sacrifices for his sons and daughters. And certainly God was not afraid to deal with Job. Obviously, this man is having a very rough time.

> **Is not thy wickedness great? and thine iniquities infinite?**
>
> **For thou hast taken a pledge from thy brother for nought, and stripped the naked of their clothing.**
>
> **Thou hast not given water to the weary to drink, and thou hast withholden bread from the hungry [Job 22:5–7].**

Eliphaz is indulging in a very mean thing here. Unfortunately there are some Christians today who indulge in this same type of thing. You see, when this tragedy struck Job, it caused many people to say, "I wonder what it is in his life?" Since they weren't able to pinpoint anything, the gossip began. Folk began to manufacture reasons. Before long they could spin quite a yarn out of a little piece of thread. That is exactly what Eliphaz is doing.

He has already accused Job of acting as if God might derive some benefit from his good behavior. Now he turns around and tells Job that his wickedness couldn't be greater. Eliphaz thinks he had just better tell Job all the things of which he is guilty. He is guessing, because none of these things are true. It is pure gossip. But look at the accusations he levies against Job.

Such treatment cannot help Job. It puts Job on the defensive. Instead of leading Job to defend God, it leads Job to defend himself. If Job becomes convinced that he is not guilty of these false accusations,

then it leads him to think that God certainly must have made a mistake and that there is something wrong with God. That is the alternative way of thinking about it. The accusations of Eliphaz lead Job to this kind of defense.

Listen to the stories the gossips tell about Job. They make him sound like a real Mr. Scrooge!

> **But as for the mighty man, he had the earth; and the honourable man dwelt in it.**

> **Thou has sent widows away empty, and the arms of the fatherless have been broken.**

> **Therefore snares are round about thee, and sudden fear troubleth thee;**

> **Or darkness, that thou canst not see; and abundance of waters cover thee [Job 22:8–11].**

Eliphaz implies that these are the things Job has done, and now the word is getting out. He goes on to warn Job that God is on high and takes note of all these things.

> **Is not God in the height of heaven? and behold the height of the stars, how high they are! [Job 22:12].**

"Job, you have been doing these things as if God doesn't see you, but God does see you. Although you thought you were getting by with it, it is obvious now that you didn't get by with it." The entire argument rests upon the premise that Job has some secret sin in his life which nobody knows but God, and now God is dealing with him in judgment. This is the explanation for his illness and all the tragedy that has happened to him—according to the argument of Eliphaz.

He thinks Job conceives of God as One who does not know what is going on.

> **And thou sayest, How doth God know? can he judge through the dark cloud?**

> **Thick clouds are a covering to him, that he seeth not; and he walketh in the circuit of heaven [Job 22:13–14].**

"Job, you don't see Him, but He sees you and knows about you."

> **Hast thou marked the old way which wicked men have trodden?**
>
> **Which were cut down out of time, whose foundation was overflown with a flood:**
>
> **Which said unto God, Depart from us: and what can the Almighty do for them? [Job 22:15–17].**

It is always the same old argument which we heard at the beginning. He rests everything upon some experience that he has had. He can say, "I have seen the wicked."

Now Eliphaz gives a gospel plea here, but it is something which Job didn't need, because he occupied a redeemed relationship. He could say, "I know that my redeemer liveth" (Job 19:25).

> **Acquaint now thyself with him, and be at peace; thereby good shall come unto thee [Job 22:21].**

That is a marvelous, wonderful invitation, but it does not apply to Job. It is like many of the invitations given in churches today—there sits a congregation of redeemed folk (at least they think they are saved), and an invitation for salvation is given. It is almost meaningless in such circumstances and borders on the ridiculous. To ask Job to accept Christ is not the answer to his problem.

"Acquaint now thyself with him, and be at peace" is a gracious invitation and a good invitation. It is the invitation which God gives to us. The Lord Jesus said the same thing in the New Testament, "Come unto me, all ye that labour and are heavy laden, and I will give you rest" (Matt. 11:28). Eliphaz said this was the way to have peace with God. Also Paul says, "Therefore being justified by faith, we have peace with God through our Lord Jesus Christ" (Rom. 5:1).

"Thereby good shall come unto thee" is true also. However, we must remember that "good" means what will be good for us. Sometimes that means discipline when we need it.

Receive, I pray thee, the law from his mouth, and lay up his words in thine heart.

If thou return to the Almighty, thou shalt be built up, thou shalt put away iniquity far from thy tabernacles [Job 22:22–23].

These men just keep harping on the one theme: "Job, there is some secret sin in your life. Deal with it and turn to God." They are treating him as if he is not even related to God at all.

Then shalt thou lay up gold as dust, and the gold of Ophir as the stones of the brooks.

Yea, the Almighty shall be thy defence, and thou shalt have plenty of silver.

For then shalt thou have thy delight in the Almighty, and shalt lift up thy face unto God [Job 22:24–26].

Eliphaz is assuming that God is Job's enemy, but God is not Job's enemy. This is an attitude which is still one of the greatest deterrents in the preaching of the gospel. Men are sinners—this should be made very clear—but God today is not at enmity with this world. God is *reconciled* to this world. You and I don't need to do anything to reconcile God; Christ did this for us. God is reconciled and has His arms outstretched to a lost world, saying, "You can come to Me, but you must come My way. You must come by the One who told you 'I am the way, the truth, and the life. No man cometh unto the Father but by Me.'" If you come His way, you can come with boldness into the presence of God. God will meet you with a great welcome and abundance of spiritual blessing. Eliphaz is not representing God accurately, as you can see. Neither is he any help or comfort to Job.

CHAPTERS 23 AND 24

THEME: Job's seventh answer

This is the seventh time that Job answers his friends, and he expresses a deep longing for God. He would like to present his case before God. He is beginning to sense that he is in the sieve of God's testing and that God will bring him through his trials.

> **Then Job answered and said,**
>
> **Even today is my complaint bitter: my stroke is heavier than my groaning [Job 23:1–2].**

Job says, "You fellows see my condition, and you have heard my complaint. Actually, my condition is worse than it looks, and it is worse than I can tell you."

> **Oh that I knew where I might find him! that I might come even to his seat! [Job 23:3].**

Job has a longing to come into the presence of God. It would be wonderful if his friends knew how to bring him into the presence of the throne of grace. He doesn't need a throne of judgment; he has already been there. And he has already been to the woodshed for discipline—there is no question about that. Now somebody needs to bring him into the presence of God.

> **I would order my cause before him, and fill my mouth with arguments [Job 23:4].**

Job says that he wants to go into the presence of God because he wants to defend himself. My friend, no one can go into God to defend himself. We all must go before God to plead guilty before Him. Every one

of us is guilty. We will find that when Job does get into the presence of God, he will not defend himself. He will change his tune altogether.

> **I would know the words which he would answer me, and understand what he would say unto me [Job 23:5].**

Job wonders what God would say to him. He wonders where he can find Him. I can assure you that any man who has that longing for God in his heart is going to find Him. God will meet him.

> **Will he plead against me with his great power? No; but he would put strength in me.**

> **There the righteous might dispute with him; so should I be delivered for ever from my judge.**

> **Behold, I go forward, but he is not there; and backward, but I cannot perceive him:**

> **On the left hand, where he doth work, but I cannot behold him: he hideth himself on the right hand, that I cannot see him [Job 23:6–9].**

God is not found by running around here and there. He is near, nearer than a hand, nearer than breathing. He is right close to you. Job says he has been running up and down trying to find God.

> **But he knoweth the way that I take: when he hath tried me, I shall come forth as gold [Job 23:10].**

Now a little light is beginning to break on the soul of Job: "I am being tested for a purpose. I don't know what it is, and I don't understand it, but God is using this in my own life."

Friend, have you discovered in your own heart and in your own life that trouble will strengthen the fiber of your faith? Haven't you found that it has given you a moral character that you never had before? Have you experienced God's strength and comfort in the time of the storm?

You know that God has never promised that we would miss the storm, but He has promised that we would make the harbor. And that is good enough for me.

> **My foot hath held his steps, his way have I kept, and not declined.**
>
> **Neither have I gone back from the commandment of his lips; I have esteemed the words of his mouth more than my necessary food [Job 23:11–12].**

Job has had a desire for the Word of God and apparently has been following God's Word. Here again is where God will teach us. Job did not understand or did not correctly interpret the Word of God. You know that some of the lessons in the Word of God cannot be learned just by studying them. They are learned by experience. Many of God's truths must be taught to us in that way.

As Job's answer continues through chapter 24, we see that he gets a little long-winded.

Eliphaz gave him the invitation, "Acquaint thyself with Him." So Job expressed his desire to find God. Job knows Him as Redeemer—he has called Him that. But he doesn't understand what is happening to him, and he needs the comfort and the help and the light from heaven, which has not been forthcoming from his friends.

Eliphaz had made a stab at trying to ferret out the secret sin which he thought was in the life of Job. The effect this has had upon Job is that it has put him even more on the defensive. In fact, it causes him now to raise another question: "Why is God so exacting with me? He apparently condones the actions of others who are really sinners and who are out in the open with their sins." This is the thrust of his argument in chapter 24.

> **Why, seeing times are not hidden from the Almighty, do they that know him not see his days?**
>
> **Some remove the landmarks; they violently take away flocks, and feed thereof [Job 24:1–2].**

Job now lists the open sins of other people. Some are dishonest. They remove the landmarks from the land.

> **They drive away the ass of the fatherless, they take the widow's ox for a pledge.**
>
> **They turn the needy out of the way: the poor of the earth hide themselves together [Job 24:3–4].**

They are not honest in their dealings, and they take advantage of other people, even those who are in need.

> **They reap every one his corn in the field: and they gather the vintage of the wicked [Job 24:6].**

The corn crop of the wicked makes just as many bushels to the acre as does the crop of the righteous. Job is asking, "Why does this happen?"

They have committed murder, they have robbed, they have committed adultery; yet this whole evil group is permitted to go down to the grave like all others.

> **Drought and heat consume the snow waters: so doth the grave those which have sinned [Job 24:19].**

Not only do they go down to the grave like others, but it seems that they are immune from justice in this life. In fact, it looks as if they are actually favored. Job looks at his own condition—he is sick and destitute, and he looks over at the wicked and sees them getting along nicely. He says, "I just don't understand it. I want to know why I am ferreted out, why I am the one who is being treated in this way."

> **And if it be not so now, who will make me a liar, and make my speech nothing worth? [Job 24:25].**

Job's friends have not helped him. In fact, they have given him another cause for complaint.

As the pastor of churches and in my ministry I have heard one question, I would be willing to say, almost a thousand times: "Why did God let this happen to me?" One hears it over and over again. That is what Job is asking here. Why did God let this happen to me? Job's premise is: "I am such a fine fellow and that crowd over there is wicked, so why me?" It is the same question that comes into the minds of many people. Job does not understand God, and we will find that Job doesn't understand himself, either. And yet Job has a great faith in God with the limited knowledge that he has.

CHAPTER 25

We are now going to have the final word from Bildad. Fortunately, it is brief. I think the light is beginning to dawn on Bildad. He is a very thoughtful and intelligent man. Perhaps he is beginning to think, *If Job is guilty, why doesn't he break under all this bombardment of argument that we have given to him?* He has still maintained his integrity. He stood up against it. Remember that Bildad is the traditionalist. He believes God follows certain laws. Things have been done this way for a thousand years, so why would there be a change? He is the scientist who pours life into the test tube, and says, "See, this is what happens every time." The Law of God is that He will punish sinners. And yet he wonders why Job doesn't break if he is a guilty sinner.

There are men today, both theologians and scientists, who speak so learnedly, especially about the creation of the earth. They seem to know exactly what God did under certain circumstances two billion years ago. We have a whole brainwashed generation, but I am, perhaps, one of the biggest skeptics you have ever known. This gross assumption of knowledge is simply not justified. My friend, they don't even know what is going to happen tomorrow, so how can they speak with such authority about what happened two billion years ago? I think they are simply kidding themselves and those who listen to them. I get a little weary of them all. Does anyone really know exactly what the first chapter of Genesis means? I think that if Moses were here today and could hear some of these scientific explanations, he would smile and say, "My, what those boys have learned since I wrote Genesis! They seem to know more than I knew about it."

Both Bildad and our contemporary intellectuals need to remember that God's ways are past finding out.

Then answered Bildad the Shuhite, and said,

Dominion and fear are with him, he maketh peace in his high places [Job 25:1–2].

He has an exalted notion of God, which is good.

> **Is there any number of his armies? and upon whom doth not his light arise? [Job 25:3].**

A better translation would be, "Whom doth not his light pass?" In other words, God is the Supreme One.

> **How then can man be justified with God? or how can he be clean that is born of a woman? [Job 25:4].**

Now here is a good question. It is a question he should have asked at the beginning. Although he has asked the right question, he doesn't have the right answer.

> **Behold even to the moon, and it shineth not; yea, the stars are not pure in his sight [Job 25:5].**

Well, we have been to the moon now, and we have found that it is a pretty dirty place. It is covered with dust and dirt, volcanic ash—not a nice place to have a picnic. It is not as romantic up there as it is down here when the moon is shining and you're out with your girl for the first time. Mars seems to be no cleaner. The stars are not pure in His sight.

> **How much less man, that is a worm? and the son of man, which is a worm? [Job 25:6].**

There are those who don't like to face that. I like it. People today talk about us having come from a worm. We haven't *come* from a worm, friends; we *are* worms. That is what we are now in God's sight.

How can a man who is born of woman be clean in God's sight? That's the question. It is a good question. It is the supreme question. Bildad did not have the answer. Only the Lord Jesus Christ has the answer to that question.

CHAPTERS 26—31

THEME: Job's eighth answer

This is Job's longest speech. It includes chapters 26 through 31. Job professes his faith in God his Creator, and we begin to see his real problem.

> But Job answered and said,
>
> How hast thou helped him that is without power? how savest thou the arm that hath no strength?
>
> How hast thou counselled him that hath no wisdom? and how hast thou plentifully declared the thing as it is? [Job 26:1–3].

"Bildad, you don't have an answer for me. Zophar, you didn't have the answer. Eliphaz, your answers didn't help me. You all had a lot of talk but no answers." They all have said many things that were good, but they were of no direct meaning nor did they communicate anything to Job, because none of them could answer the question of the *why* of Job's suffering.

> To whom hast thou uttered words? and whose spirit came from thee? [Job 26:4].

"To whom hast thou uttered words?" You have finally come up with the right question, Bildad, but you have no answer; so who has been helped by all this talk?

Now Job really launches into his discourse. In it he will lay his soul bare. He has a lot to say, and some of it is really great. He moves into the area of the Creation and God as the Creator.

Dead things are formed from under the waters, and the inhabitants thereof.

Hell is naked before him, and destruction hath no covering.

He stretcheth out the north over the empty place, and hangeth the earth upon nothing [Job 26:5–7].

Much has been made of the fact that He "stretcheth out the north over the empty place." Folk have attempted to point out that there is a void in the north, that there are no stars in a certain place in the north. In fact, it was called a "hole in the north." However, since we have these very powerful telescopes, and especially the radio telescopes, we find that we cannot point a telescope in any direction in God's universe without finding it filled with stars—other universes. Job is saying that God reached out in space and covered it—He can cover the empty place.

Also space is a creation of God. Here is one star which God has created. Billions and billions of light years over yonder is another star, and God has also created that one. What keeps them from rubbing together or banging into each other like cars do on our freeways today? Well, God put space between them. What is space? Maybe some people would answer, "Nothing." Friend, it is something. I don't know what it is, but it is something, and God created it to hold heavenly bodies apart. It is like a lubricant that He uses to keep the universes from banging into each other.

Listen to the apostle Paul. "For I am persuaded, that neither death, nor life, nor angels, nor principalities, nor powers, nor things present [that's time], nor things to come [that's future], Nor height, nor depth [that's space], nor any other creature, shall be able to separate us from the love of God, which is in Christ Jesus our Lord" (Rom. 8:38–39). "Nor any other creature" is literally "nor any other created thing." Space is one of God's creations. Friend, that gives us something to turn over in our minds. What is space?

It takes a long time to go to the moon. What is all this expanse

between the earth and the moon? Don't tell me it is nothing, because it is *something*. What is it? I don't know; I'm no authority on that. I simply know that we call it space, God created it, and it is out there serving His purpose.

He "hangeth the earth upon nothing." Who in the world told Job that? Remember that Job lived back in the age of the patriarchs, and yet this man knew that this earth is hanging out in space. That God suspends the huge ball of earth in space with nothing to support it but His own fixed laws was a concept unknown to ancient astronomers.

Job understood that He "hangeth the earth upon nothing." There is no foundation under it. If it fell, what direction would it go? We talk about gravity, but that is a pulling down toward the center of the earth. When you get out far enough into space, there is nothing pulling on anything. So where is down and where is up? And what keeps it hanging there in space? We get an answer in Colossians 1:17: "And he is before all things, and by him all things consist." The word *consist* is the Greek *sunsitemi*, meaning "to hold together." By Christ it all is held together. We are moving now into a great section of the Book of Job.

Job had a tremendous view of God as the Creator. Out there on the ash heap he was able to look at the stars at night, and he had spent time doing that in the past.

> **By his spirit he hath garnished the heavens; his hand hath formed the crooked serpent.**
>
> **Lo, these are parts of his ways: but how little a portion is heard of him? but the thunder of his power who can understand? [Job 26:13–14].**

God has garnished the heavens with stars. Probably the "crooked serpent" that Job mentions is a constellation out in the heavens. He is calling attention to the greatness of God as He is revealed in the heavens by His wonderful creation.

We see that Job knew God as a Creator; Job understood Him as a

Redeemer; but Job did not know God as a Sustainer and the One who loved him. He did not understand that God would not let anything happen to him unless it would minister to him.

JOB CONDEMNS THE WICKED

We are approaching some of the really basic material of this book. The Book of Job reaches right down where we are, into the center of our lives. Beneath the suffering which Job went through there is a great lesson for him to learn. That is the reason I say that the main lesson of the Book of Job is not why believers suffer. Suffering is not the main issue of the book. Behind it all is the great teaching of repentance, repentance in a child of God.

When a sinner comes to God, is he to repent? Paul told the jailer at Phillipi, ". . . Believe on the Lord Jesus Christ, and thou shalt be saved, and thy house" (Acts 16:31). Paul made no mention of repentance, but repentance is in that word believe, because when a sinner turns to Christ in faith, he also turns away from sin. In the case of the Philippian jailer, it was probably his idolatry from which he turned. That would be his repentance. Turning to Christ is the important part.

Many a child of God today and many a lost sinner are self-sufficient. Anyone who is self-sufficient needs to repent, as this book will reveal. This is the great lesson of the Book of Job.

> **Moreover Job continued his parable, and said,**
>
> **As God liveth, who hath taken away my judgment; and the Almighty, who hath vexed my soul;**
>
> **All the while my breath is in me, and the spirit of God is in my nostrils;**
>
> **My lips shall not speak wickedness, nor my tongue utter deceit [Job 27:1–4].**

I would like to give a translation here which may be helpful in bringing out the meaning. "As God liveth, who hath taken away my right,

and the Almighty, who hath embittered my soul (all the while my breath is in me, and the Spirit of God is in my nostrils); my lips shall not speak unrighteousness, nor my tongue utter deceit." Job makes it very clear that he is undaunted and that he is determined. Zophar hasn't answered, and so Job keeps on talking, and he says, "I will never admit the charges that you three so-called friends have brought against me." On the contrary, he says:

> **God forbid that I should justify you: till I die I will not
> remove mine integrity from me [Job 27:5].**

He is stubborn, isn't he? All his friends have been able to do is to make him more and more defensive. In defending himself there is no brokenness of spirit, no humility of mind. It makes it look as if God is the One who is unrighteous, while Job is perfectly all right. He says, "I will not remove mine integrity from me."

> **My righteousness I hold fast, and will not let it go: my
> heart shall not reproach me so long as I live [Job 27:6].**

Listen to him! These friends have not led him to self-judgment but have only ministered to a spirit of self-defense. Job is vindicating himself. You see, God is not on the scene here. Job is being rather foolhardy in all this because before it is over, we will see that Job is down in dust and ashes before God.

There is a lesson for us to learn in all this. I certainly will grant that many things which his friends said to Job were truths. Also I am of the opinion that these men had the best intentions. Although they said things that were true, I don't think that they had *the* truth. They talked about experience and tradition and legality, but they never gave Job the truth. Having failed to do that, they built up the man's ego.

Let me repeat this because it is so important. They thought that Job had committed some secret sin, and they were trying to bring it out into the open. Job had not committed some great, secret sin, and he knew that they were wrong. Since they were wrong, Job assumed he was right. That is where Job made his mistake. The fact that his friends

were wrong in no way made Job right. Job should have been in the presence of God where there would have been a brokenness of spirit. One of the purposes of trouble in our lives is to lead us into that brokenness of spirit before God.

Someone has said that trouble is like the sun. The sun shining on wax will melt it. The same sun shining on clay will harden it. That is the way trouble affects different people. Some will respond with a broken spirit. They just melt before the presence of God. Job isn't to that place yet. He is hard now, hard as nails in his own integrity.

"My righteousness I hold fast, and will not let it go: my heart shall not reproach me so long as I live." This is the position and condition of a lot of church members today. They feel exactly the same way. The assurance of salvation is wonderful to have, but, my friend, you can be a hardboiled sinner, thinking you have assurance of salvation, when all you have is a great big ego. You feel that you have it made. Well, Job thought he had it made, and he is going to find out otherwise very shortly.

> **Let mine enemy be as the wicked, and he that riseth up against me as the unrighteous [Job 27:7].**

Job is putting everyone who disagrees with him over on the other side. They are his enemies. They are wicked and they are unrighteous. I tell you, that is a dangerous position for any man! Now Job is going to talk about the wicked and what is going to happen to them. Job will give a little lecture now. In the midst of all his own trouble, this man is going to give a lecture about the wicked.

> **For what is the hope of the hypocrite, though he hath gained, when God taketh away his soul?**
>
> **Will God hear his cry when trouble cometh upon him?**
>
> **Will he delight himself in the Almighty? will he always call upon God?**
>
> **I will teach you by the hand of God: that which is with the Almighty will I not conceal [Job 27:8–11].**

Job is saying that the wicked may prosper but God will eventually judge them.

> **The rich man shall lie down, but he shall not be gathered: he openeth his eyes, and he is not.**

> **Terrors take hold on him as waters, a tempest stealeth him away in the night.**

> **The east wind carrieth him away and he departeth: and as a storm hurleth him out of his place [Job 27:19–21].**

Riches will make no difference. If a man has been wicked, his life will go out like a flame that is blown out, like a candle blown out by a wind coming through a window. The time will come when—

> **Men shall clap their hands at him, and shall hiss him out of his place [Job 27:23].**

Can you remember a time when millions saluted Musolini? There came a day when people actually walked across his dead body and that of his paramour as they lay in the mud after their execution. The wicked shall be judged. There will come an end to their wickedness and to the glory they seem to have. But that doesn't answer Job's problem.

Job is still full of words.

POEM OF CREATION

He continues his discourse with one of the most beautiful poems of creation that you can find anywhere. It may not seem like poetry to us, but it is Hebrew poetry and it is beautiful. He deals with things that are absolutely wondrful. If we were studying poetry, I would spend a long time here.

> **Surely there is a vein for the silver, and a place for gold where they fine it.**

> Iron is taken out of the earth, and brass is molten out of the stone.
>
> He setteth an end to darkness, and searcheth out all perfection: the stones of darkness, and the shadow of death [Job 28:1-3].

God has put silver and gold and iron and precious stones into the earth. It is difficult to find these things. I personally do not think that men have found the vastness of the treasures that are really in this old earth on which we live. I think this chapter is saying that clearly. It also suggests that there are precious stones which have never yet been discovered, which might be more valuable than the diamond.

> The flood breaketh out from the inhabitant; even the waters forgotten of the foot: they are dried up, they are gone away from men.
>
> As for the earth, out of it cometh bread: and under it is turned up as it were fire [Job 28:4-5].

Not only does the earth turn up precious stones, but also it produces food—bread for us to eat.

> The stones of it are the place of sapphires: and it hath dust of gold.
>
> There is a path which no fowl knoweth, and which the vulture's eye hath not seen:
>
> The lion's whelps have not trodden it, nor the fierce lion passed by it [Job 28:6-8].

The birds fly over the earth and its mountains. There are veins of minerals down in the earth that the birds fly over and know nothing about, neither can the vulture see them. There must be precious stones and veins of riches and wealth which are completely unknown and untapped.

> **He putteth forth his hand upon the rock; he overturneth
> the mountains by the roots [Job 28:9].**

God can cause the earthquake. He can change the topography of the land. He can expose those veins of riches in the earth that He wants to have exposed.

> **He cutteth out rivers among the rocks; and his eye seeth
> every precious thing.**
>
> **He bindeth the floods from overflowing; and the thing
> that is hid bringeth he forth to light [Job 28:10–11].**

Job has been talking about the minerals and the precious stones in the earth. There are things which are of even more value: wisdom and understanding. Job knows that God has placed the minerals in the earth, but where is the source of that precious commodity—wisdom?

> **But where shall wisdom be found? and where is the
> place of understanding?**
>
> **Man knoweth not the price thereof; neither is it found in
> the land of the living.**
>
> **The depth saith, It is not in me: and the sea saith, It is
> not with me [Job 28:12–14].**

Job is telling his friends that they have not found wisdom.

I would like to voice an opinion on the basis of this passage. I do not believe that all of this probing of the ocean floor and space and every crevice in the earth is going to tell man anything relating to real wisdom and real knowledge concerning the origin of the earth. Man cannot find it there. He will not learn how it came into existence nor who put it into existence.

> **It cannot be gotten for gold, neither shall silver be
> weighed for the price thereof [Job 28:15].**

We have paid billions of dollars to bring back rocks from the moon. Those are mighty expensive rocks, friend. But they are not telling man what he would like to know.

> **It cannot be valued with the gold of Ophir, with the precious onyx, or the sapphire.**
>
> **The gold and the crystal cannot equal it: and the exchange of it shall not be for jewels of fine gold.**
>
> **No mention shall be made of coral, or of pearls: for the price of wisdom is above rubies [Job 28:16–18].**

The wisdom that Job hoped his friends would bring to him is a wisdom beyond the understanding of man.

> **The topaz of Ethiopia shall not equal it, neither shall it be valued with pure gold [Job 28:19].**

Even the Bureau of Standards just can't evaluate it.

> **Whence then cometh wisdom? and where is the place of understanding?**
>
> **Seeing it is hid from the eyes of all living, and kept close from the fowls of the air.**
>
> **Destruction and death say, We have heard the fame thereof with our ears [Job 28:20–22].**

We have heard about it, but even death ought to tell us *something*. It ought to tell us that there is something on the other side, and it ought to tell us that there is something we don't know. Men just step through the doorway of death, my friend, and they are not able to get word back to us. Houdini, the great magician, left a code with his wife before he died so that he could communicate with her after he was gone. Spiritualist after spiritualist came to Mrs. Houdini, claiming to have a message from him. She would say, "Give me the code." Not one of them

was able to come up with the code, which means that no one heard from Houdini after he died. We just don't get word back from over there. That should tell us that there is something which we do not know today.

He goes on to say something very interesting:

When he made a decree for the rain, and a way for the lightning of the thunder [Job 28:26].

For many years the critics said this was an incorrect statement; that everyone knows you see the lightning before you hear the thunder. But after it was discovered that sound waves do not travel as fast as light waves, they realized that the lightning is the flash from the crash of the thunder that takes place. How amazing that the writer of the Book of Job knew that it was the "lightning of the thunder"!

And unto man he said, Behold, the fear of the LORD, that is wisdom; and to depart from evil is understanding [Job 28:28].

Job's friends were not able to probe this man's problem at all. We are going to see his secret sin revealed, but it is not anything that his friends suspected.

He is suffering from a bad case of perpendicular "I-itis." This is a very bad disease. It is a case when the little pronoun "I" becomes so important that all we can talk about is "I, I, I ." We find that Job is filled with pride. This shows us that even a good man needs to repent. We will find in this chapter of twenty verses that Job uses the personal pronouns "I" or "me" fifty-two times. Mark them in your Bible. You will be amazed. Job is wrapped up in himself. That is his big problem. We will see how it had affected his life. It affects the life of anyone when he gets all wrapped up in himself. Someone has said, "When you're wrapped up in yourself, it makes a mighty small package."

This chapter does not contain any form of a confession by Job. It is really his boasting. He has "I" trouble. There are many of us who have it too. The perpendicular pronoun is the hub of the wheel of life for all

of us. Everything is a spoke that goes out from us. We see no brokenness of spirit. There is not that broken and contrite heart, no admission
of guilt, no confession, no feeling of guilt or failure.

His friends were not able to help him. They failed to see the real
problem. They didn't know Job, and they didn't know themselves, and
they certainly didn't know God. They believed that God sent trouble to
Job only as a punishment, and they thought Job was just holding out.
They roughed him up and were miserable comforters to him. Each one
used a different approach, and yet they all came to the same conclusion.

We can sum up the methods of his friends. Eliphaz was the voice of
experience. He used what would be called today the psychological approach. This is the approach of the power of positive thinking. It
adopts a cheerful attitude. Bildad was the traditionalist, and he used
the philosophical approach. That would be the approach of several of
the seminaries today. They use the philosophical approach, but that
doesn't help anyone. Zophar was a religious dogmatist. He thought he
knew all about God. He sounds like some of us fundamentalists, by the
way. All of us would fall into the category of one of these friends. As we
have seen, not one of his friends had been able to help him.

Now I do want to say on Job's behalf, as we move into this chapter,
that he was a "perfect" man according to the standard which God had
set up, which was sacrifice. He was a very wealthy man. He had all
that it took to make this life agreeable. He had what it took to make him
important in the world. We have seen that he was a religious man. He
feared God. He had a concern for his children. He didn't put up a false
front. He could be weighed on the scale of God's balance and not be
called a hypocrite. So the insinuation of his friends was base and low.
He was a genuine saint of God, a quickened soul, a child of God. His
earthly cup of bliss had been full and running over. Then why should
this man suffer?

Actually, the suffering is only incidental—although Job would
never have told you that. The suffering in Job is about as important as
the fish in the Book of Jonah, in which the real problem is between
Jonah and Jehovah. Here the real problem is between Job and Jehovah.
Even Satan, the enemy, is secondary.

The real problem is Job. He did not know himself, and he did not know God. Socrates has said, "Know thyself." That is important. Job didn't know himself. He was self-righteous and self-sufficient. He received all kinds of compliments from people, and there was a little of the self-adulation. There was a spiritual egotism in this man's life. We will see this clearly when God confronts him.

Job now is going to tell us about himself. He reviews his past. Chapter 29 is Job's "This is my life."

Moreover Job continued his parable, and said,

Oh that I were as in months past, as in the days when God preserved me [Job 29:1–2].

Job reminds me of a little tea party I heard about:

I had a little tea party
This afternoon at three.
'Twas very small—
Three guests in all,
Just I, Myself and Me.
Myself ate all the sandwiches,
While I drank up the tea.
'Twas also I who ate the pie
And passed the cake to Me.
—Author unknown

When his candle shined upon my head, and when by his light I walked through darkness [Job 29:3].

Those were the good old days for Job.

As I was in the days of my youth, when the secret of God was upon my tabernacle [Job 29:4].

Here is a man who from his youth served God.

> When the Almighty was yet with me, when my children were about me;
>
> When I washed my steps with butter, and the rock poured me out rivers of oil;
>
> When I went out to the gate through the city, when I prepared my seat in the street! [Job 29:5-7].

He was prosperous. Everything he touched turned to gold. Not only was he a prosperous man, but he was also a man of influence.

> The young men saw me, and hid themselves: and the aged arose, and stood up.
>
> The princes refrained talking, and laid their hand on their mouth.
>
> The nobles held their peace, and their tongue cleaved to the roof of their mouth [Job 29:8-10].

The children would run and hide from him because he was such a great man. The old men would rise when they saw him coming. They would take off their hats and bow to him. When he came, all the others quit talking. Even the princes and the nobles were silent. They waited for Job to speak. Nobility didn't speak in his presence unless he asked them to do so.

> When the ear heard me, then it blessed me; and when the eye saw me, it gave witness to me [Job 29:11].

He was voted the most valuable citizen by the city clubs of Uz in Chaldea. He was the outstanding citizen of the town.

> Because I delivered the poor that cried, and the fatherless, and him that had none to help him [Job 29:12].

He provided pensions for the aged. He helped the poor.

> **The blessing of him that was ready to perish came upon me: and I caused the widow's heart to sing for joy [Job 29:13].**

He took care of the widows. My, this man was thoughtful!

> **I put on righteousness, and it clothed me: my judgment was as a robe and a diadem [Job 29:14].**

Job was adorned with good works. And people came to him for advice.

> **I was eyes to the blind, and feet was I to the lame [Job 29:15].**

He was chairman of the board at the blind school, and he was a benefactor of the crippled children's home. My friend, this man Job was outstanding! How we need citizens like this.

> **I was a father to the poor: and the cause which I knew not I searched out [Job 29:16].**

He made a thorough investigation before he gave to a cause. This is something which many believers do not do today. Job supported only that which he knew to be a worthy cause.

> **And I brake the jaws of the wicked, and plucked the spoil out of his teeth [Job 29:17].**

He believed in civic righteousness and law and order. He was influential enough to bring it to pass. What a man he was!

> **Then I said, I shall die in my nest, and I shall multiply my days as the sand.**
>
> **My root was spread out by the waters, and the dew lay all night upon my branch.**

**My glory was fresh in me, and my bow was renewed in
my hand [Job 29:18–20].**

Job said to himself, "I've got it made. I have everything I want for re-
tirement. I'm going to die in my nest. I'll multiply my days as the sand
and live to a ripe old age." I tell you, he thought he had everything. He
had a wonderful family. He had good health. One can't think of anything that Job did not have.

> **Unto me men gave ear, and waited, and kept silence at
> my counsel.**
>
> **After my words they spake not again: and my speech
> dropped upon them.**
>
> **And they waited for me as for the rain; and they opened
> their mouth wide as for the latter rain [Job 29:21–23].**

All the group sought out his advice. Before they would make a decision, they would contact Job and ask his advice. The governor of the
state and the supreme court would talk things over with Job before they
made a decision. I tell you, he was an outstanding man of great influence. They would hang on every word that Job said.

> **I laughed on them, they believed it not; and the light of
> my countenance they cast not down.**
>
> **I chose out their way, and sat chief, and dwelt as a king
> in the army, as one that comforteth the mourners [Job
> 29:24–25].**

Job sat at the very top of the totem pole of life. He dwelt in honor, affluence, and influence. He was a plutocrat and a tycoon. He was an ideal
man, the goal toward which humanity is striving today. He lived the
good life. He knew what abundant living really was.

But Job lived in a fool's paradise. He was in a Cinderella world; and
when the clock struck midnight, his chariot turned into a pumpkin.

Remember what he said in chapter 3: "For the thing which I greatly feared is come upon me, and that which I was afraid of is come unto me. I was not in safety, neither had I rest, neither was I quiet; yet trouble came" (Job 3:25–26). The bomb fell on his nest. He had dreaded something like this. He had feared that all of this material substance could be wiped out and taken from him in a moment, and it was. He had nothing to fall back on. Even his friends didn't cushion his fall. In fact, they made him fall with a terrible, resounding crash.

Job has been putting on his self-righteousness. Listen to him again in verse 14: "I put on righteousness, and it clothed me: my judgment was as a robe and a diadem." Fifty-two times he has used "I" and "me." We hear no confession, no admission of failure. We see nothing of a broken and contrite spirit in Job.

Chapter 30 continues his description of his present wretchedness and suffering.

> **But now they that are younger than I have me in derision, whose fathers I would have disdained to have set with the dogs of my flock [Job 30:1].**

"I have told you how it used to be, but now—now these young scoundrels come around and throw rocks at me. They have no use for me. Let me tell you about the fathers of these kids. I wouldn't even have hired them to watch over my flock."

> **Yea, whereto might the strength of their hands profit me, in whom old age was perished?**
>
> **For want and famine they were solitary; fleeing into the wilderness in former time desolate and waste [Job 30:2–3].**

He goes on to deride these scoundrels who now have no use for him.

> **And now am I their song, yea, I am their byword.**

They abhor me, they flee far from me, and spare not to spit in my face [Job 30:9–10].

They are making up dirty little ditties about Job, and they ridicule him in song. He knew what it was to be the object of derision led by young hoodlums.

I don't know about you, but I am tired of listening to Job. First he was boasting about the outstanding man he had been. Now he is courting sympathy. "I was such a great fellow and now look at me." And who is to blame for this, my friend? Why, God is to blame.

There are lot of Christians in that same position today. It is possible to be blaming God but to do it in a very pious way. "I had all those blessings. I was so active. I did kind things for people. But look at me now." Well, whatever it is that has happened, it is because God is good, never because God is not good. Whatever happens is because God is working out something beneficial in the life of a believer.

Job finally says,

My harp also is turned to mourning, and my organ into the voice of them that weep [Job 30:31].

His singing voice is the *harp.* All he can sing now is the "Desert Blues." The *organ* is his speaking voice, and he says all it can do is weep. He has a tear in his voice all the time. That is his condition now. He is asking for sympathy and certainly is a man to be pitied.

However, you will notice that there still is no brokenness of spirit. God has been put at a great disadvantage in this man's life. He is a proud man. He justifies himself instead of justifying God. In fact, he *blames* God. What is the problem of Job? It is pride. It is the same thing that caused Satan to fall. It was the sin in the Garden of Eden. It is that awful thing that eats like a cancer into the human heart. That awful sin of pride is there in the hearts and lives of all of us.

JOB CONCLUDES HIS SELF-DEFENSE

Now chapter 32 concludes Job's lengthy defense. It has been quite a slugging match! The three friends of Job, lined up against him, have

attempted to beat him down into admitting that he had committed a great sin. Their logic, as we have seen, is that God would not have permitted him to suffer so if he had not committed some terrible sin.

After going three rounds with him, they gave up, which is evident by the fact that the last man, Zophar, did not answer Job. When he did not step forward to make his rebuttal, Job continued to speak. Believe me, they had teed him off, and he came out of his corner fighting.

In defending himself, he must accuse God—it boils itself down to that. He is implying that God is wrong in punishing him. Probably the most foolish thing any person can do is to justify himself, inasmuch as God must impute sin. The minute you begin to justify yourself, God immediately will have to point the finger at you and say what you are. Real wisdom, and the correct position, is to condemn ourselves utterly and to cast ourselves upon God. When we do that, God becomes our justifier. There is nothing but *wrath* for the self-righteous. And there is nothing but *grace* for the self-judged. This is very important for us to remember in our own lives.

Humility is a quality that we admire and look for in others. A clipping from the *New York Times* regarding a contemporary boxing match underscores this fact: ". . . Ability to wear the trappings of humility is an occupational requirement in certain lines of work, particularly in politics and championship boxing. He who scorns them invites the vengeance of an outraged public. . . . We like our champions humble. After they have flattened some poor gaffer for our amusement, we want them to come to the microphone like Joe Louis and Rocky Marciano and say, 'He put up a good fight.' Muhammad Ali outrages us by coming to the microphone and calling a bum a bum."

May I say to you, it is a characteristic of human nature to be proud. Boxers are not the only ones guilty of pride. It just may be that they are a bit more brazen about it, but pride characterizes the human family.

The Book of Job is teaching us that when we come before God, He wants us to be real before Him. We can't put up a defense for ourselves. There is no possible use in trying to build ourselves up as if we were some great person or had done some great thing. Nothing is more sure than that God will break down every such type of arrogance. The Day of the Lord will be against everything high and lifted up. So it is

wisdom for us to take the low and broken place today, for it is the low place that gives us our best view of God and His salvation.

There is a great deal of this "coming forward" in response to an altar call which does not lead to real salvation because of the fact that some folk come in pride.

I wonder if you have ever noted in the Word of God the references to this matter of being contrite and how God approves of it. "The LORD is nigh unto them that are of a broken heart; and saveth such as be of a contrite spirit" (Ps. 34:18). You see, real repentance involves taking that position. We need to recognize that just as David did. Listen to him in that great penitential psalm when he made his confession: "The sacrifices of God are a broken spirit: a broken and contrite heart, O God, thou wilt not despise" (Ps. 51:17). My friend, when you come to God to do business with Him, you do not come to God to trade with Him on equal terms and turn in your little goodness to Him. We need to recognize that we approach God through contrition. This is taught all through the Bible.

"For thus saith the high and lofty One that inhabiteth eternity, whose name is Holy; I dwell in the high and holy place, with him also that is of a contrite and humble spirit, to revive the spirit of the humble, and to revive the heart of the contrite ones" (Is. 57:15). This matter of being humble and contrite is not a problem for the politicians and the boxers alone; it is a problem for all believers today, especially those who are in the Lord's service. I think that we can say that egotism and self-conceit are more detestable when they show themselves in the servants of the Lord Jesus Christ, the One who ". . . made himself of no reputation, and took upon him the form of a servant . . ." (Phil. 2:7). How unlike Him is pride in the lives of those who name His name and say they are believers. To reveal a hateful, unsubdued, self-displaying Christian profession and Christian service is atrocious. And in this final section Job is not very attractive.

Job has been doing a good job of patting himself on the back. He has told what an outstanding, influential, good man he was and has made a play for sympathy for his present condition. As he concludes his discourse in this chapter, he is still claiming that he is a very good fellow.

I made a covenant with mine eyes; why then should I
think upon a maid? [Job 31:1].

Job makes it very clear that he had lived a clean life. He didn't run
around and chase women. He wants them to know he has not been
guilty of ordinary sensual sins.

For what portion of God is there from above? and what
inheritance of the Almighty from on high?

Is not destruction to the wicked? and a strange punishment to the workers of iniquity? [Job 31:2–3].

He is still pointing his finger at others who commit such things, and
he says they are to be judged. He cannot see why he should be judged
so severely when he is such a wonderful fellow. He is about to break his
arm patting himself on the back.

Doth not he see my ways, and count all my steps?

If I have walked with vanity, or if my foot hath hasted to
deceit;

Let me be weighed in an even balance, that God may
know mine integrity [Job 31:4–6].

He is boasting of his integrity. Well, he is going to come into the presence of God before long, and he is going to really *see* himself—then he
won't see much integrity.

If my step hath turned out of the way, and mine heart
walked after mine eyes, and if any blot hath cleaved to
mine hands;

Then let me sow, and let another eat; yea, let my offspring be rooted out.

If mine heart have been deceived by a woman, or if I
have laid wait at my neighbour's door.

Then let my wife grind unto another, and let others bow down upon her.

For this is an heinous crime; yea, it is an iniquity to be punished by the judges [Job 31:7–11].

He says that if he has been unfaithful or untrue, let his wife be taken from him. He hasn't lived in sin as some other folks do. And I believe that all these things Job is saying are completely accurate. He was really a good man. But he has this terrible blind spot: pride. His friends have led him into a defense of himself and he just can't let up. He must boast about his goodness.

We see this same sort of thing today among Christians. For a child of God to boast and to live in pride is just as bad as getting a gun and murdering someone. Pride among Christians is one of the things that causes our churches to be so cold today. People sit in the pews and think that they are just all right. My friend, if you are in Christ Jesus, you are saved, but regardless of who you are, your life is not measuring up to God's standard—and neither is mine.

If I did despise the cause of my manservant or of my maidservant, when they contended with me;

What then shall I do when God riseth up? and when he visiteth, what shall I answer him? [Job 31:13–14].

Job was an employer, and he says that he was good to his employees. He was a capitalist who was good to labor. There should be more who could say that today. Of course, in our time the shoe is on the other foot, and labor is not too nice to the consumer today. Anyway, the point is that Job could say that he had been considerate of others.

If I have withheld the poor from their desire, or have caused the eyes of the widow to fail;

Or have eaten my morsel myself alone, and the fatherless hath not eaten thereof;

(For from my youth he was brought up with me, as with
a father, and I have guided her from my mother's womb;)

If I have seen any perish for want of clothing, or any
poor without covering;

If his loins have not blessed me, and if he were not
warmed with the fleece of my sheep;

If I have lifted up my hand against the fatherless, when I
saw my help in the gate:

Then let mine arm fall from my shoulder blade, and
mine arm be broken from the bone [Job 31:16-22].

Job had certainly helped the poor. He had a poverty program long before anyone else ever had one. He took care of the orphans. He goes
over all this ground again. He is boasting of all the things that he has
done. I believe he really did them, too, but he is lifted up with pride
about it. That is where he is in trouble. He is constantly saying, in
effect, "I have been so good that God is unjust in treating me as He is.
God is wrong."

My friend, we need to get to the place where we can praise His
name above everything and can see ourselves down in the dust before
Him.

If I rejoiced at the destruction of him that hated me, or
lifted up myself when evil found him:

Neither have I suffered my mouth to sin by wishing a
curse to his soul [Job 31:29-30].

Job says that he didn't rejoice when his enemy stubbed his toe and had
trouble. He was not spiteful.

If I covered my transgressions as Adam, by hiding mine
iniquity in my bosom:

Did I fear a great multitude, or did the contempt of families terrify me, that I kept silence, and went not out of the door?

Oh that one would hear me! behold, my desire is, that the Almighty would answer me, and that mine adversary had written a book.

Surely I would take it upon my shoulder, and bind it as a crown to me [Job 31:33–36].

He says he has not done anything in secret. He wishes his enemies would write out what they think of him, and he would be glad to wear it like a necktie or like a crown on his head so everyone could see it. He would walk up and down the streets and say, "Look, this is what my enemy says about me, and it is all *praise* for me." How Job is boasting! He has discussed everything about his life, but he has not made a confession of his pride.

Job is righteous in his own eyes, but Job is not righteous before God.

CHAPTERS 32—37

THEME: The discourse of Elihu

There is a crowd standing around listening to these men talk. When Job is finished with his discourse, it is one of the members of this audience, Elihu, who picks up the discourse and carries on from then until God breaks into the discussion. During this time a storm gathers on the horizon. By the time we get to the end of Elihu's discourse, the storm breaks upon the group, and they all run for cover. Only Job is left there in the storm. It is then that God will deal with Job personally.

Now the three friends of Job are through. They fade into the distance. Frankly, I heave a sigh of relief. I am thankful they are through talking, and I hope they've gone home.

To all intents and purposes, Job has won the debate. But he hasn't won. Here stands a young man with something to say. He hasn't opened his mouth so far, which is unusual for a young man, but this is a very intelligent young man.

So these three men ceased to answer Job, because he was righteous in his own eyes [Job 32:1].

That, of course, is accurate–Job was righteous in his own eyes.

The three friends had not been able to give an answer to Job. They failed to meet his need in all their reasonings and in all their arguments. Eliphaz was the one who had referred to experience. Zophar was the legalist. Bildad put his arguments on the basis of human authority. None of them had been able to come up with a solution for Job. They had said many things that were true—they came up with a number of great truths—but they did not answer Job's problem. At the end of it all, Job remained righteous in his own eyes.

There was a value in this controversy. It is important for us to see that when two parties are divided over any issue, they can never reach an understanding unless there is a brokenness and a submissiveness

and a willingness to be subdued and not to contend for self on the part of one or both of the parties involved. We find a lot of high-mindedness today, inside and outside the church, which is the cause of a great many of the problems that we have today. Job was a high-minded man. He has been touchy and tenacious and easily provoked, but his friends have been equally so. They have not been able to come to any kind of an understanding.

I think we ought to say on behalf of the friends of Job that they found no answer because there was no answer. Only God can answer a self-righteous individual. We will find that finally God did break in with an answer for Job. To anything else the unbroken heart can find a ready reply, but not to God, of course. Job's friends had no answer.

Now Elihu is going to break into the conversation. He doesn't have an answer for Job, but he comes closer than the others had come. And I do think that he prepares the way for God finally to break in upon this scene. Then God will give Job some information from "Headquarters" that all of us need.

Notice that Elihu is a Buzite (descended from Buz, Gen. 22:21), evidently a tribe of Arabs.

> **Then was kindled the wrath of Elihu the son of Barachel the Buzite, of the kindred of Ram: against Job was his wrath kindled, because he justified himself rather than God [Job 32:2].**

Elihu speaks because he is angry, and he is angry on two counts. Job had spent his time justifying himself rather than God. This meant that he was actually saying, "God is wrong. God has made a big mistake with me." This aroused the anger of Elihu.

> **Also against his three friends was his wrath kindled, because they had found no answer, and yet had condemned Job [Job 32:3].**

This was the second reason for his anger. The friends had not been able to put their finger on Job's real problem, and yet they were condemning Job.

**Now Elihu had waited till Job had spoken, because they
were elder than he [Job 32:4].**

Things apparently were different in that day from what they are today.
A modern young man would already have broken into the conversation. We find in our society that little Willie has center stage. I have
noticed this with my grandson. I tell you, he is on center stage, up
front all the time. We listen to him, and I'm not sure that that is wise.

**When Elihu saw that there was no answer in the mouth
of these three men, then his wrath was kindled [Job
32:5].**

Elihu had waited. He thought these older men would come up with
something very wise. I can remember when I was a young preacher
that I was frightened to death of the gray heads in the congregation
because I thought they knew a great deal—probably much more than I
did. However, I soon learned that length of days did not always indicate knowledge or depth of wisdom.

**And Elihu the son of Barachel the Buzite answered and
said, I am young, and ye are very old; wherefore I was
afraid, and durst not shew you mine opinion.**

**I said, Days should speak, and multitude of years
should teach wisdom [Job 32:6–7].**

Notice this interesting comment:

**But there is a spirit in man: and the inspiration of the
Almighty giveth them understanding [Job 32:8].**

Elihu doesn't have the same position with the Holy Spirit that believers have today. Apparently the Holy Spirit did not *indwell* believers in
the Old Testament, but He did come *upon* certain men for the perfor-
mance of certain functions. For example, Bezaleel was filled with the
spirit of God (Exod. 31:2–3) who gave him the skill and wisdom to
make the articles of furniture for the tabernacle. The spirit of God

came upon many men in the Old Testament. David prayed, ". . . Take not thy holy spirit from me" (Ps. 51:11), which would indicate that the Holy Spirit could depart from an Old Testament believer. There is no teaching in the Old Testament that men were indwelt by the spirit of God. Elihu recognizes that only the inspiration of the Almighty can give understanding to man. This means that there is only one sure authority, and that is the Word of God.

> **Great men are not always wise: neither do the aged understand judgment [Job 32:9].**

The "inspiration of the Almighty giveth them understanding"—he recognizes that only God could provide an answer in Job's case.

Elihu is preparing the way for God to answer. Although he himself does not really have the answer, he recognizes that these other men did not have the answer either.

> **Therefore I said, Hearken to me; I also will shew mine opinion.**
>
> **Behold, I waited for your words; I gave ear to your reasons, whilst ye searched out what to say.**
>
> **Yea, I attended unto you, and, behold, there was none of you that convinced Job, or that answered his words. [Job 32:10–12].**

This, of course, is absolutely true.

> **Lest ye should say, We have found out wisdom: God thrusteth him down, not man [Job 32:13].**

It disturbed Elihu because he felt that these men should have been able to answer Job. It disturbed him because Job stands vindicated, and in this position he feels very cocky and self-confident.

The literal meaning of the word *contrite* is "bruised." Now it is true that Job has been battered and bruised. He has been in the ring with Satan, and he has had three rounds with his friends. This man Job is

coming out bruised, there is no question about that. But contrition comes from within a man. It is grief and penitence for sin.

David understood that "the sacrifices of God are a broken spirit: a broken and a contrite heart, O God, thou wilt not despise" (Ps. 51:17). Job had been bruised, but he still was not contrite. However, God is not through with him yet.

Only God has the answer for self-righteousness, pride, and arrogance. Sometimes people come to me with this story: "I have a son who has gone to college, and he knows everything now. How can I answer a boy like that?" The answer is that only God can deal with a son who thinks he knows it all.

The minute that you and I become self-righteous we can be sure of one thing: we will be brought into the ring with God, and He is going to bruise us. He must treat us in that way because it seems to require bruising to bring us to a realization of our sin and to a spirit of humility.

It was that spirit of humility which was demonstrated in the life of John Wesley. There is a somewhat humorous anecdote about his humility. It is said that Wesley was crossing a narrow bridge when he met an enemy right in the middle of it. It was impossible to pass, and his enemy drew himself up to his full height, and said, "I never give way to an ass!" Wesley looked at him for a minute, and then he answered, "Well, I always do," and he just backed off the little bridge and let the man go by. I guess that would be the best answer one could give in a case like that. Not many men would been willing to back off, but Wesley was.

When I think of a really contrite spirit, I think of the confession of Horatius Bonar. He said, "I went to God to confess my coldness, my indifference, and my pride. After I had finished, I went back again to God and I repented of my repentance." My friend, that is true contrition to repent of your repentance! You see, it is very easy for us to be proud even of our repentance.

Elihu expected Job's friends to continue the debate.

When I had waited, (for they spake not, but stood still, and answered no more;)

> **I said, I will answer also my part, I also will shew mine opinion [Job 32:16–17].**

Here we have the suggestion that it was Elihu who was the author of the book of Job. Notice that he is using "I" when he gives this explanation, and it sounds as if he were writing the book.

> **For I am full of matter, the spirit within me constraineth me. [Job 32:18].**

He is saying here that he is constrained from saying more. He really would like to say more, but he will not say it. Apparently the spirit of God held him back.

Unfortunately, many of us are high-minded. We are touchy and tenacious. We are easily provoked. We are ready to get into this business of vindicating ourselves, and we don't want anyone to rebuke us at all. There is not that softness of tone or delicacy of touch. We pour no oil on the troubled waters. We do not have that broken heart and weeping eye. We parade our own experience like Eliphaz. We indulge in a legal spirit like Zophar. We introduce human authority like Bildad. We do not demonstrate the spirit and the mind of Christ.

Remember that Proverbs 15:1 tells us that "a soft answer turneth away wrath: but grievous words stir up anger." Most of us forget that— or perhaps I am just talking about myself.

THE CREATOR INSTRUCTS THROUGH DISCIPLINE

Now Elihu has something to say.

> **Wherefore, Job, I pray thee, hear my speeches, and hearken to all my words. Behold, now I have opened my mouth, my tongue hath spoken in my mouth [Job 33:1–2].**

He is going to insist on several great truths.

My words shall be of the uprightness of my heart: and my lips shall utter knowledge clearly.

The spirit of God hath made me, and the breath of the Almighty hath given me life [Job 33:3–4].

My friend, this is a great truth. God is my Creator.

Elihu is going to speak by the spirit of God. He says that the other men haven't been able to answer Job, and now he is going to try.

Peter, in his epistle, wrote, "If any man speak, let him speak as the oracles of God . . ." (1 Peter 4:11). I would like to write these words in the chapels of every seminary in this country. If a minister is not speaking for God (I don't mean to be crude, but I am going to say it anyway), he should shut up! He has no business talking. After I had been speaking in the San Francisco Bay area, a man said to me, "You sound very dogmatic." I said, "Yes, I'm glad it got through to you that I am dogmatic." "Well," he said, "there are other ways of looking at the Bible." I discovered that he was a legalist. He said, "Have you ever thought that there might be another explanation?" I told him, "Yes. There was a time when I thought there were several ways a man could come to God. But after many years of study I have come to the conclusion that the way God saves is by grace, and I am dogmatic about it. I am dogmatic about quite a few things in the Word of God—because the Word of God is dogmatic. I am dogmatic about the deity of Jesus Christ, that He is the Son of God. I am dogmatic about the fact that He is virgin born, that He performed miracles, that He died a substitutionary death, that He rose bodily from the grave, that He ascended to heaven, that He is seated today at God's right hand, that He is the living Christ right now, and that He is coming back someday. Brother, I am dogmatic!" The fellow looked at me and said, "Then I guess there is no use in my talking with you." I said, "If you have a different viewpoint, you would be wasting your time, I can assure you." My friend, let me say it as Peter said it, "If any many speak, let him speak as the oracles of God." Of course there is such a thing as dogmatic ignorance. But the point I am making is that when you are quoting the Bible, if you are not sure it is the Word of God, then you have nothing to say at all. Unbelief is always dumb. It has nothing to say. I don't mean that it

doesn't talk—it talks a great deal. But any ministry is powerless, valueless, and fruitless unless a man is speaking as the oracles of God.

> **If thou canst answer me, set thy words in order before me, stand up.**
>
> **Behold, I am according to thy wish in God's stead: I also am formed out of the clay [Job 33:5–6].**

Job has been wanting a man to represent him before God. This young fellow, Elihu, is willing to do that. He says, "I'm made of the same clay you are made of." He wants to stand as a mediator between Job and God. Obviously, he is not the man, but it reveals the great need for the incarnation of our Lord. He must be a Mediator so He must be God, but He must also be of the same clay as we are.

> **Behold, my terror shall not make thee afraid, neither shall my hand be heavy upon thee.**
>
> **Surely thou hast spoken in mine hearing, and I have heard the voice of thy words, saying,**
>
> **I am clean without transgression, I am innocent; neither is there iniquity in me [Job 33:7–9].**

Elihu had been listening to all the preceding conversation and had heard that Job considered himself innocent and that he found fault with God. Now Elihu tells Job that God is greater than man and not responsible to man.

> **Behold, he findeth occasions against me, he counteth me for his enemy.**
>
> **He putteth my feet in the stocks, he marketh all my paths.**
>
> **Behold, in this thou are not just: I will answer thee, that God is greater than man [Job 33:10–12].**

He makes the great statement that God is greater than man. It is a simple statement; yet it is great because so many folk take the place of God. Many Christians propose to tell you why certain things happen. Some Christians speak as if they have a private line into heaven—they get the latest right off the wire. I doubt that sincerely. There is a great deal that none of us know.

Why dost thou strive against him? for he giveth not account of any of his matters [Job 33:13].

Job needs to understand that God didn't need to report back to any board. He is not responsible to any group, nor is He subject to public opinion.

My friend, God is not responsible to either you or me. He doesn't have to give an answer to us. He is not accountable to us. Some people say, "Oh, why does God let this happen to me?" I don't know why, my friend; all I know is that God is not accountable to you. He doesn't have to tell you the reason why. He doesn't have to tell me the reason why. He has asked me to trust Him. He has never promised that He would take me out of the darkness, but He says, "Put your hand in My hand and I will lead you *through* the darkness." He has not promised to explain everything to us. He has asked us to trust Him!

For God speaketh once, yea twice, yet man perceiveth it not.

In a dream, in a vision of the night, when deep sleep falleth upon men, in slumberings upon the bed [Job 33:14–15].

We must recognize that since we have the completed Bible, we do not need to trust any dream that we have had. However, way out on the frontier where the Gospel has not gone, I think you will find that God still uses this method.

Then he openeth the ears of men, and sealeth their instruction,

**That he may withdraw man from his purpose, and hide
pride from man [Job 33:16–17].**

The problem with Job was that he had an awful disease—it was cancer
of the spirit: pride. Oh, the proud heart of man! And I see it in my own
life. Do you see it in yours? How we need to grovel in the dust and put
on sackcloth and ashes because of the kind of folk we are. Elihu says
here that God instructs men through discipline.

Job's false reasoning is a very simple thing. He did not understand
the character of God; so he did not understand God's dealings with
him. But God *was* dealing with Job, and He wanted to "hide pride"
from him. He wanted to take pride out of that man's life. Job was a
good man; he was a great man. But he was a low-down sinner just like
you are and just like I am. Because we are sinners, pride creeps into
our lives. For example, we get angry with individuals who dare criti-
cize us. God "withdraweth not his eyes from the righteous . . ." (Job
36:7). We are in His hands, and we are under His eye continually. We
are the objects of His deep and tender and unchanging love, but we are
also the subject of His wise and moral government. He doesn't want
spoiled brats as His children!

Lo, all these things worketh God oftentimes with man,

**To bring back his soul from the pit, to be enlightened
with the light of the living [Job 33:29–30].**

God often instructs men through discipline. God uses it to deliver his
soul from going into "the pit."

**Mark well, O Job, hearken unto me: hold thy peace, and
I will speak.**

**If thou hast any thing to say, answer me: speak, for I
desire to justify thee.**

**If not, hearken unto me: hold they peace, and I shall
teach thee wisdom [Job 33:31–33].**

God still wants to do the same thing for believers today. We need to consider the exhortaton given us in Hebrews: "For consider him that endured such contradiction of sinners against himself, lest ye be wearied and faint in your minds. Ye have not yet resisted unto blood, striving against sin. And ye have forgotten the exhortation which speaketh unto you as unto children, My son, despise not thou the chastening of the Lord, nor faint when thou art rebuked of him" (Heb. 12:3–5). Then drop down to verse 11: "Now no chastening for the present seemeth to be joyous, but grievous: nevertheless afterward it yieldeth the peaceable fruit of righteousness unto them which are exercised thereby" (Heb. 12:11). There are three distinct ways in which we may meet the chastening of our Heavenly Father: (1) We can *despise* it as though His hand and His voice were not in it. We can ignore God. (2) We may *faint* under it. When we do that, it is real defeat. Job had had both these reactions, by the way. But what are we to do? (3) We are to be exercised by it so that it will produce the fruit of righteousness in our lives. God does permit trouble to come to His own, and He chastens every son whom He receives. That is the great purpose that is behind all that has been happening to Job. God is going to bring it to a tremendous consummation.

GOD NEVER DOES WICKEDLY

Now as we continue listening to Elihu in chapter 34, notice that for a man of his day he has real spiritual insight. He certainly is defending God in this matter. Up to this point the Lord was at a distinct disadvantage, because it looked as if the Lord were either punishing Job because of some great sin in his life, or, if there were no great sin in his life, then God was unjust. It looked as if the Lord would have to prove Job to be a great sinner, but God didn't have to do that, as we shall see.

If Job could only have been shown by his friends that God was dealing with him—not in the sense of punishing him for his sin, but that God was using all of these instruments in attempting to take pride out of his life and reduce him to a plane where he could trust God, where he could respond even as little Samuel did, ". . . Speak; for thy servant heareth" (1 Sam. 3:10). Job was so busy defending himself that he couldn't see that God was using circumstances, people, the Sabeans,

storms, even Satan himself as God's marvelous agencies to bring this man to a very gracious and a very wise end. God's mercy was actually being displayed. His mercy endureth forever! Job had lost sight of that, which removed him from God.

We need to recognize that God moves in our lives as believers. We get occupied with men and things and circumstances, and we look at them in reference to our lives instead of walking with God. We do not live above our circumstances, but under them, and then our circumstances weigh us down.

A wonderful man of God, who is now with the Lord, was my friend in the ministry. He used to kid me and say, "McGee, your trouble is that you live under your circumstances and you don't live on top of them." Although he was kidding me, what he said was true. Actually, God permitted me to have cancer, and now I can see a purpose in it. Don't misunderstand me. I'm not being pious and saying, "I praise the Lord for my cancer." I do not. I'd get rid of it in the next minute if I could. But the point of it is that I recognize God has used this in my life.

When we let circumstances come between us and God, God is shut out, and as a result of that we lose the sense of His presence. We get to the place where there is worry and distress instead of peace in our souls, and we do not feel His fatherly hand upon us. We become fretful and impatient and irritable and faultfinding. We get far away from God and out of communion with Him. We do not see the hand of God in all our circumstances. All the while He wants to bring us back to Himself in brokenness of heart and humbleness of mind. This is the "end of the Lord," that for which He is striving in your life and in mine.

Elihu is the one who concludes man's attempted ministry to Job. Now Job will experience the direct ministry of God. There will be a threefold effect on him: it will change his relationship to God and to his friends and to himself. My friend, we all need to be changed within ourselves. The Lord will chasten for this purpose. God doesn't mind doing that, because it will bring us to that place of humility before God so that He can use us. God uses chastening for this purpose in our lives.

Furthermore Elihu answered and said,

Hear my words, O ye wise men, and give ear unto me, ye that have knowledge [Job 34:1–2].

Now Elihu turns to the three friends and has a word for them.

For the ear trieth words, as the mouth tasteth meat [Job 34:3].

As we taste something that we eat with our tastebuds, so also the ear tastes—it tastes words or "trieth words." Music is delightful to the ear; we taste it with our ears.

Let us choose to us judgment: let us know among ourselves what is good [Job 34:4].

Just as we like to taste something good, let's hear something that is good.

For Job hath said, I am righteous: and God hath taken away my judgment [Job 34:5].

Job has been saying that he is righteous and that God hasn't given him a fair trial. In other words, God is not fair to me.

Should I lie against my right? my wound is incurable without transgression [Job 34:6].

Job maintains that he has an incurable disease and didn't do anything to deserve it.

What man is like Job, who drinketh up scorning like water? [Job 34:7].

Job despised the chastening of the Lord. He felt that God had no right to treat him so. This attitude removed him far from God. Then he began to faint under the chastening—we are not to faint when we are rebuked of Him. God is doing all this to accomplish a good purpose in our lives.

Which goeth in company with the workers of iniquity, and walketh with wicked men [Job 34:8].

Job has joined the protesters outside of heaven. He is in company with the workers of iniquity and walks with wicked men. It is as if he is marching up and down with a placard that reads: "God is wrong and I am right." A lot of folk are doing that. Job has joined with those who are in rebellion against God.

For he hath said, It profiteth a man nothing that he should delight himself with God [Job 34:9].

Job might as well have said, "I have been serving God and being a nice little boy, and I expected to have a Sunday School pin. At Christmas I expected God to put a nice gift in my stocking. Instead, God put ashes in my stocking, and I don't think that God has been very nice to me in doing that." That was the attitude of Job, and it is the attitude of a lot of Christians today.

Therefore hearken unto me, ye men of understanding: far be it from God, that he should do wickedness; and from the Almighty, that he should commit iniquity [Job 34:10].

Again he is saying that *God* does not do *wrong*. Remember that Paul asked, "Is there unrighteousness with God? God forbid" (Rom. 9:14). My friend, it may sound ugly to say this, but if you say that God is wrong then you are wrong. God is always right and you and I are the ones who are always wrong. No matter what God does, He is right. He doesn't have to report to you or me. He doesn't need to ask our permission to do something.

It is interesting today to find people who are willing to let criminals have their freedom to live as they choose, but they don't want God to have the freedom to run the universe the way He chooses. My friend, He will run it right, and He is not bound by your standards or my standards.

> **Yea, surely God will not do wickedly, neither will the Almighty pervert judgment [Job 34:12].**

Now that is something you can write down in your little book and keep it there. God does not do wickedly. He will not permit a wrong act. If you want to go back in the Old Testament and find fault with God for getting rid of the Amorites, that is your privilege. But that doesn't make God wrong. He was right. Maybe you say, "I just don't see it." Well, maybe I don't either. But I know that God extended His grace to them for four hundred years and gave them time to repent, and only after that period of time did He wipe them out. God is always right. Reason from *that* point.

You see, our whole system of human thinking is based on reasoning from experience to the truth, and that is the reason so few of us ever arrive at truth. God reasons from truth, and He *is* the truth. The Lord Jesus said, ". . . I am . . . the truth" (John 14:6). When Pilate asked, ". . . What is truth? . . ." (John 18:38). *Truth* was standing right before him. Jesus is the Truth. We need to learn to reason from the truth to experience, which is what God does.

> **Who hath given him a charge over the earth? or who hath disposed the whole world?**
>
> **If he set his heart upon man, if he gather unto himself his spirit and his breath [Job 34:13–14].**

The point is that God has a care, God has a concern for man.

> **Surely it is meet to be said unto God, I have borne chastisement, I will not offend any more [Job 34:31].**

If God has chastened you, then you ought to learn your lesson and not continue in your old way. Maybe God is attempting to develop something in your life. He won't let anything happen to you unless it accomplishes a worthy purpose.

> **That which I see not teach thou me: if I have done iniquity, I will do no more [Job 34:32].**

If you have done iniquity, and you know the purpose of God's chastening is to get you away from sin, then for goodness' sake, learn the lesson and turn from the sin.

> **Let men of understanding tell me, and let a wise man hearken unto me.**

> **Job hath spoken without knowledge, and his words were without wisdom [Job 34:34–35].**

What is said of Job could be said of most of us. We do a lot of talking, but a great deal of it is "without knowledge" and "without wisdom." We are living in a day when we have what are known as rap sessions. I meet with a lot of groups, especially young people, who want to have a rap session. I welcome the opportunity, but I hear a lot of asinine and foolish things said. It wasn't only Job who spoke without knowledge. A lot of folk today speak without knowledge and some of them have a Ph.D. degree. A degree is no guarantee of knowledge or wisdom.

> **My desire is that Job may be tried unto the end because of his answers for wicked men.**

> **For he addeth rebellion unto his sin, he clappeth his hands among us, and multiplieth his words against God [Job 34:36–37].**

What Elihu is saying is that he hopes God will try Job until Job will be able to defend God instead of defending himself.

GOD IS TEACHING JOB A LESSON

Elihu spake moreover, and said,

Thinkest thou this to be right, that thou saidst, My righteousness is more than God's? [Job 35:1–2].

The minute Job says that he is right and that he is suffering in spite of being right, God must be wrong. That is the inference one must draw from that type of reasoning.

> **Look unto the heavens, and see; and behold the clouds which are higher than thou.**
>
> **If thou sinnest, what doest thou against him? or if thy transgressions be multiplied, what doest thou unto him? [Job 35:5–6].**

This is the question that Job was raising. He was saying, "My little life is not affecting God." The wonder of it all is that it does affect Him. A sin is something that is almost infinite. Abraham sinned in the case of that little handmaid Hagar, and the world is still paying for that sin in the conflicts of the Middle East. He took the Egyptian at the suggestion of Sarah, but Abraham and Sarah were wrong. How wrong were they? The results of their wrong have gone on for four thousand years. Sin is an awful thing, and it does affect God.

> **Thy wickedness may hurt a man as thou art; and thy righteousness may profit the son of man [Job 35:8].**

You are always a witness, my friend. You are a *preacher*, regardless of who you are. The mother of a drunken man asked me to talk to her son. Once when he went wobbling down the street, I detoured him into my study. I told him what a low-down, dirty ingrate he was and how he disgraced his mother, breaking her heart. He just sat there and took all of it. Then I said, "You preach by your life. You are a preacher." He stood up to fight me. I could call him anything in the world except a

preacher. Well, my friend, you are a preacher! Your wickedness will hurt somebody, and your righteousness may help somebody.

By reason of the multitude of oppressions they make the oppressed to cry: they cry out by reason of the arm of the mighty.

But none saith, Where is God my maker, who giveth songs in the night [Job 35:9–10].

That is so wonderful! It is God who gives songs in the night. The only place of happiness is with God. Have you ever noticed the expression, "Blessed be the God and Father of our Lord Jesus Christ . . ." (Eph. 1:3) What does that word *blessed* mean? It means "happy." God is happy and He wants us happy. When Moses came down from the mountain, his face was shining because there was now forgiveness. There was now sacrifice for sin, and God would deal with man in grace.

John writes, "And these things write we unto you, that your *joy* may be full" (1 John 1:4). He is the One who gives songs in the night. The night clubs have songs. They are the blues and you *pay* for them and you have a headache the next morning. It is God alone who can bring happiness to you. That is so important. And Elihu had learned that way back there in the patriarchal period.

After we finish the discourse of Elihu, we will find that God will break through to Job. A storm will come up and break over Job, and out of that storm God will speak to him. It is through the storms of life that God wants to speak peace to you and me. Oh, let us not let circumstances come between our souls and our God!

GOD IS THE GREAT TEACHER

Elihu also proceeded, and said,

Suffer me a little, and I will shew thee that I have yet to speak on God's behalf [Job 36:1–2].

Elihu is defending God. He has—as all of us have—a limited knowledge of God. We are dealing with an infinite God, and we don't have all the answers.

That is the difficulty for a great many people today. A man said to me, "I can't believe." I asked, "What is it that you can't believe? Do you believe that Jesus died on the cross and that He rose again?" Yes, he believed that. "Well," I said, "then why can't you trust Him?" "There is so much else—creation, Jonah, Noah, and the miracles." Also he had all kinds of personal problems. Then he challenged me, "You make the statement that we are unbelievers because of our sin, but I *want* to be a believer." May I say that he is committing the real sin, and it is this: he is letting what he *doesn't* know disturb him in what he *does* know. My friend, if you know enough to trust Christ, these other things will adjust themselves.

Let me illustrate. As I write, I am sitting in a chair. Now there is a great deal about this chair that I do not know. To begin with, I don't know who made it. I don't even know the company that made it. I don't know much about the materials in the chair—what kind of wood it is, what kind of covering it has. I really know very little about this chair. But, friend, I know enough to sit down in it and trust myself to it.

Do you know that Christ died for you? Do you know He rose again? All right, then *trust* Him as your Savior. These other doubts will take care of themselves in time, I can assure you. If it were necessary for me to know more about this chair, I think I could find out. But all I need to know is just enough to sit in it. I know very little about an airplane, and I am even fearful when I get on one, but I walk aboard, sit down, and trust myself to it. That is all God asks us to do when we trust Christ. Too many of us let what we don't know disturb what we do know.

Now Elihu is quite limited in knowledge, as we shall see.

I will fetch my knowledge from afar, and will ascribe righteousness to my Maker [Job 36:3].

Paul said the same thing years later. He asked, ". . . Is there unrighteousness with God?" His answer was, "God forbid" (Rom. 9:14). God is righteous in all that He is and does.

Although Elihu is ascribing righteousness to God, he is also making it clear that God is so far removed from man that, actually, man

cannot know Him. There is an element of truth in that, by the way. But what is it today that is separating us from God? Notice what Elihu is saying.

> **For truly my words shall not be false: he that is perfect in knowledge is with thee [Job 36:4].**

That is, only God has perfect knowledge.

> **Behold, God is mighty, and despiseth not any: he is mighty in strength and wisdom.**
>
> **He preserveth not the life of the wicked: but giveth right to the poor.**
>
> **He withdraweth not his eyes from the righteous: but with kings are they on the throne; yea, he doth establish them for ever, and they are exalted [Job 36:5–7].**

The whole sense of what he is saying is simply that God is far removed from us. He is separated from us, and we cannot communicate with Him because He is so far from us. Elihu is *wrong* in that. And many folk today are wrong in that concept.

Listen to the words of Isaiah concerning that which separates man from God. It is not because of distance. It is not because God is great and we are small. It is not because He is infinite and we are finite. "But your iniquities have separated between you and your God, and your sins have hid his face from you, that he will not hear" (Isa. 59:2). He continues to describe their situation: "For your hands are defiled with blood, and your fingers with iniquity; your lips have spoken lies, your tongue hath muttered perverseness. None calleth for justice, nor any pleadeth for truth: they trust in vanity, and speak lies; they conceive mischief, and bring forth iniquity" (Isa. 59:3–4). God says these are the things that separate man from God.

Today there is no reason for you and me to be separated from God. The sin question has been settled forever. There is one Mediator between God and man, the man Christ Jesus, and today we can come to

God through Him. The great cry of Job was for someone to make a connection for him with God. Elihu came nearer to this than anyone else, but he didn't make it. That is the reason God finally broke in on Job.

Then Elihu states that God is the great Teacher.

> **Behold, God exalteth by his power; who teacheth like him?**
>
> **Who hath enjoined him his way? or who can say, Thou hast wrought iniquity? [Job 36:22–23].**

Elihu felt that he couldn't communicate with Him, but he does say this: "No one can teach like God." As you know, this was the thing that marked out the Lord Jesus Christ when He came to this earth. He was the greatest Teacher of all. Even His enemies said, ". . . Never man spake like this man" (John 7:46). The teaching of the Lord Jesus is the greatest teaching that the world has ever known right down to this present hour.

It is a strange thing that people today who reject the Lord Jesus Christ still try to use His teachings. They talk about loving your neighbor. They talk about mercy. They talk about the Sermon on the Mount. You don't hear them trying to foster the teachings of Plato or Aristotle even though they were smart boys. No, the Lord Jesus still stands as the greatest Teacher. Elihu asked, "Who teacheth like Him?"

ELIHU CONCLUDES

Chapter 37 concludes what Elihu has to say. I am going to lift out only three verses from this final chapter:

> **Fair weather cometh out of the north: with God is terrible majesty.**
>
> **Touching the Almighty, we cannot find him out: he is excellent in power, and in judgment, and in plenty of justice: he will not afflict.**

**Men do therefore fear him: he respecteth not any that
are wise of heart [Job 37:22–24].**

Again, he is inferring that God is so far removed from man that we just
cannot communicate with Him. He is way up yonder, and we are way
down here. However, we have already seen that it is not the greatness
and majesty of God that has separated man from Him; it is man's sin.

This chapter clearly shows us that Elihu cannot be a prophet or a
mediator for Job. That is one of the reasons that I have never special-
ized in counseling. If you want to know the truth, I don't know enough
to be a counselor. I feel that a man who is going to pose as a counselor
is sitting in the place of God. The friends of Job tried to be his coun-
selors. They were trying to take the place of God in this man's life.
Their problem was that their own knowledge was not adequate. We
need to recognize counseling for what it is. It arises out of the experience and wisdom of another human being. The great breakdown in
counseling is that no one is all-knowing, no one is omniscient. No
counselor can know all the facts or have all the wisdom that is necessary.

As you know by now, I have cancer and it is necessary for me to
have a good doctor. I wanted the very best, and I have a wonderful
doctor. The thing I like about him is that he is not all-knowing or all-
powerful. He isn't afraid to tell me, "I don't know." I like that. It makes
him a human being. He does not put himself into the place of God. He
is a fine Christian and is attempting to serve the Lord, so he doesn't try
to usurp God's place.

Elihu really almost tried to move into God's place. He wanted to be
a mediator for Job. But he breaks off here with the fact that he really
doesn't know God as he should. He doesn't know how to approach
God, and he is far removed from Him. That is why it is necessary for
God to break through.

You will notice in verse 22 that he gives a little weather report. He
says, "Fair weather cometh out of the north." Why do you suppose he
said that? I think that during most of the discourse of Elihu a storm
was forming over the horizon. It grew darker, and the storm began to

advance. The wind was probably howling, and a few drops of rain were beginning to fall. It became a formidable storm, and the people were running for shelter. I think that after he finished his discourse, Elihu also took off and ran for shelter.

Job was left, alone.

CHAPTERS 38—42

THEME: Jehovah and Job

We last saw Job left all alone. Now God breaks in on this man in his weakness. God meets him right at the point of his own inadequacy. God is so great!

JEHOVAH VS. JOB

The mark of a good teacher is that he begins where a student has left off. He will begin where the student is and will move up to where he wants to bring him. God is a teacher. He will teach Job here. The Lord Jesus Christ is also a teacher, the greatest teacher. He wants to teach us today.

Notice here as God teaches Job that He begins right where they left off—in nature. A storm is coming up, and God breaks in as the Creator. He begins there, and He will bring this man to where He wants to bring him.

The Lord Jesus also taught that way. I don't think the parables of the Lord Jesus were imagined. He would just stop and observe the lives of the people of that day, and that would be His parable. He would meet them where they were. For example, ". . . Behold, a sower went forth to sow" (see Matt. 13:3–9). There were little hills all through Palestine and, wherever He walked, He would see the sowers sowing the grain. Or, ". . . The kingdom of heaven is like unto leaven, which a woman took, and hid in three measures of meal . . ." (Matt. 13:33). That was a common experience, and Jesus had watched women do that over and over again. The Lord Jesus began his teaching where the people were, and then He brought them to where He wanted them to be.

We find this teaching principle all through the Word of God, which is the greatest teaching available to man. It begins where we are and teaches and brings us to where God wants us to be.

I tried to use this principle in my conference preaching. Whenever

I came to a different city, I would buy the paper for a few days before
the conference. Then I would begin speaking at the conference with
some reference to a local situation—the race for mayor, some famous
person visiting there, or some kind of scandal in that city. I would try
to start with a casual remark about it, probably something humorous.
Why? Because that is where the people lived.

So we find God breaking in right where Job is. I want to confess as
we come to this part of the book that if I felt totally inadequate up to
this point, now I don't even know what to say. I feel like just simply
being quiet, closing my Bible and stopping. But we cannot do that, so
we will simply read what God says, and I will make a few comments as
we go along.

JEHOVAH SPEAKS TO JOB

**Then the LORD answered Job out of the whirlwind, and
said [Job 38:1].**

God answers Job out of the whirlwind, out of that storm that has now
broken upon Job. God is speaking to him as the Creator.

**Who is this that darkeneth counsel by words without
knowledge? [Job 38:2].**

We will find that Job will finally be willing to say that he has uttered
words without knowledge. That, my friend, is an awful sin. I think we
have a lot of it today. Those talk programs on television not only commit this sin, but most of them are the most asinine things imaginable.
They accomplish nothing at all, but they make for entertainment and
are prepared by some light-headed folk. God says, "Who is this that
darkeneth counsel by words without knowledge?"

One man said he liked the dictionary because the stories in it were
so short. Well, there are a great many people who pull a few words out
of the dictionary and attempt to put them together. Whether they make
sense or not doesn't seem to be the point as long as they are using big
words.

Gird up now thy loins like a man; for I will demand of thee, and answer thou me.

Where wast thou when I laid the foundations of the earth? declare, if thou hast understanding [Job 38:3-4].

This is the verse that I have always wanted to put in the front of every book on geology, but they won't let me do it. It makes no difference whether the book was written by a Christian or a non-Christian; I think it should be put in the book. "Where wast thou when I laid the foundations of the earth? declare, if thou hast understanding." By the way, where were you? That is a good question.

What is it that holds this universe in space? And it is not standing still. You and I are on a little earth that is as unstable in itself as anything can be. There is nothing under it to hold it up. I don't even know which is under—what is down or up—as far as the universe is concerned. Why doesn't it start going in some direction? Why does it just go around and around? What keeps it going around and around? Apparently it has been doing this for millions of years. The question is, "Where wast thou when I laid the foundations of the earth?"

A geologist once took me up to a ridge in northern Arizona—I thought it was a ridge, but it was just sand. I couldn't understand why sand was piled up there. He kicked away the sand and under it was a petrified log. I asked, "My, where did this come from?" He said, "California." I said, "Who hauled it in here?" He answered, "It floated in here." Now if you look at that Arizona desert, it is hard to imagine that there was ever any water that could have floated that log. But, apparently that is what has happened. That log had floated in from California.

I asked, "When did that happen?" He said, "Well, about 250,000 years ago." And he said it like he had been there when the log arrived. Now it may be that he was right. I am not contradicting him and saying that he was wrong. I am saying that there are a lot of folk today who seem to know what took place millions and millions of years ago. God asks, "Where wast thou when I laid the foundations of the earth? declare, if thou hast understanding."

Who hath laid the measures thereof, if thou knowest? or who hath stretched the line upon it?

Whereupon are the foundations thereof fastened? or who laid the corner stone thereof [Job 38:5-6].

The Book of Job apparently comes from the period before any word of Scripture was written. God begins with Job at the point where He began with all men at that particular time—at the point of creation. Paul began at this same point when he talked about the revelation of God to all mankind. "For the wrath of God is revealed from heaven against all ungodliness and unrighteousness of men, who hold the truth in unrighteousness; Because that which may be known of God is manifest in them; for God hath shewed it unto them. For the invisible things of him from the creation of the world are clearly seen, being understood by the things that are made, even his eternal power and Godhead; so that they are without excuse" (Rom. 1:18-20).

It is all important for us to see that God was speaking to Job and to all men in that day through His creation. They were close enough to creation that there was no atheism. Instead, there was polytheism. They actually worshiped the creature rather than the Creator. This is what Paul went on to speak of in the first chapter of Romans (Rom. 1:21-23).

I am not going to attempt to develop this section here. It has to do with creation. It has to do with this physical universe that you and I live in today. And, as Paul says in Romans, creation speaks of God: the person of God, the power of God, and the wisdom of God. Creation reveals the greatness of our God. How great Thou art! This is the impression we are bound to get, as God speaks of the fact that He is the Creator and He knows much that man does not know.

When the morning stars sang together, and all the sons of God shouted for joy? [Job 38:7].

Actually, man is a "Johnny-come-lately" in God's universe. There was a joy in creation even before man was created.

My friend, if you are His son, you are going to have joy in your life.

God wants you to have joy. "Blessed be the God and Father of our Lord Jesus Christ . . ." (Eph. 1:3). Blessed! The word is *happy*. God is happy. He's joyful and He wants us to be joyful. I hope that the joy of the Lord is your portion today. He wants it to be.

There are a couple of interesting verses here:

> **Hast thou entered into the treasures of the snow? or hast thou seen the treasures of the hail,**
>
> **Which I have reserved against the time of trouble, against the day of battle and war? [Job 38:22–23].**

Some fantastic interpretations have been drawn from these verses of how snow and hail will be used in warfare, but I am not about to get out on a limb with this. I do know that snow is what defeated Napoleon. Revelation 8:7 tells us that God will use hail in one of the judgments of the earth. But here God is simply making the point to Job that His creation is beyond the understanding of man. Only God can know these things.

He goes on to talk about the starry heavens:

> **Canst thou bind the sweet influences of Pleiades, or loose the bands of Orion?**
>
> **Canst thou bring forth Mazzaroth in his season? or canst thou guide Arcturus with his sons?**
>
> **Knowest thou the ordinances of heaven? canst thou set the dominion thereof in the earth? [Job 38:31–33].**

What do we know about those tremendous stars out yonder in the heavens? I do not know how much the ancients knew about them, but apparently they knew a great deal more than we give them credit for knowing. It is my understanding that the Egyptians were able to accurately measure the distance to the sun. Therefore they must have had considerable knowledge.

Have you known God through His creation? Can you really know God through creation? I think God is making it very clear to Job that

the creation reveals His greatness. One can know about God through His creation, but creation will not bring a man to a saving knowledge of God.

Chapter 38 has shown God in His past creation. Chapter 39 will reveal God in nature—God as the sustainer of His creation. This is His revelation through His creation right at the present.

> **Knowest thou the time when the wild goats of the rock bring forth? or canst thou mark when the hinds do calve? [Job 39:1].**

God is the God of nature. Things happen in nature today because God makes them happen. Without God, nature would be dead; nothing would happen. There would be no spring, no summer, no fall, no winter, no storms, no movement in this universe. It would all come to a dead standstill if there were no Creator and Sustainer behind it. Think that one through. That is the point that God is making to this man Job. He is revealing His greatness.

> **Moreover the Lord answered Job, and said,**

> **Shall he that contendeth with the Almighty instruct him? he that reproveth God, let him answer it [Job 40:1-2].**

"Job, are you in a position to give God a lesson? Actually, Job, you have been speaking without knowledge." Job has been attempting to instruct God. He has been attempting to tell God something, and he is in no position to do that because he has been uttering words without knowledge. Now God wants an answer from Job.

> **Then Job answered the Lord, and said,**

> **Behold, I am vile; what shall I answer thee? I will lay mine hand upon my mouth.**

> **Once have I spoken; but I will not answer: yea, twice; but I will proceed no further [Job 40:3-5].**

Job says, "I should have kept quiet. Now I see I am vile." Is this the man who said that he would maintain his integrity regardless of what happened? Is this the man who declared that he was a righteous man and that therefore there must be something wrong with God to let this happen to him? This same man is now saying that he is vile.

As someone has said, if we could see ourselves as God sees us, we couldn't stand ourselves. When we get into the presence of God, we will acknowledge that we are vile.

This appearance of God to Job had a three-fold effect upon him. It had an effect upon his relationship to God, his relationship to himself, and his relationship to his friends. This is the man who has spoken without knowledge. His words were without wisdom. Now he wishes that he had kept his mouth shut. He becomes suddenly silent. He lays his hand over his mouth.

> **Then answered the Lord unto Job out of the whirlwind, and said,**
>
> **Gird up thy loins now like a man: I will demand of thee, and declare thou unto me.**
>
> **Wilt thou also disannul my judgment? wilt thou condemn me, that thou mayest be righteous? [Job 40:6–8].**

The storm breaks in all of its fury, and God speaks out of the whirlwind. He continues His appeal to Job. God is asking Job, "Are you trying to say to Me that I am wrong?" Of course, God is not wrong. Eventually Job is going to be able to say to God, "I know that thou canst do every thing, and that no thought can be withholden from thee" (Job 42:2). Job is going to come a long way.

Actually, Job is already advancing. He had not known himself but has now come to the point where he has discovered that he is vile. When a man discovers that, he has come a long way. This is the first step Job takes as he comes to God.

The Lord again appeals to Job on the basis of His creation. "Job, look around. There are a lot of things that you don't know. How can you judge Me and My moral government of this universe?"

Many folk today come up with some asinine statements concerning God. I have heard Christians say some very foolish things about the Lord. Friend, we ought to be very careful what we say about Him. We should keep our words in the context of the Word of God.

It is quite obvious that Job actually did not know God. He has uttered words without knowledge. And when the Lord breaks in upon him, He asks him some more questions.

> **Canst thou draw out leviathan with an hook? or his tongue with a cord which thou lettest down?**
>
> **Canst thou put an hook into his nose? or bore his jaw through with a thorn? [Job 41:1–2].**

"Job, what do you really know about this great monster of the sea?" Today they are making a study of the great whales off the coast of California. They are doing many things, trying to find out about them. We've come a long way since the days of Job, and we still don't know all about those big fellows that are in the water.

What do we know about dinosaurs? I have heard this whimsy about the guide in the museum who gave a lecture to the crowd. When they came to the dinosaur he said, "This dinosaur is two million and six years old." A man came up to him and said, "Wait a minute. I'll accept the two million years, but where do you get the six years?" The guide answered, "Well, when I came to work here, that dinosaur was two million years old. I've been here six years now. So the dinosaur is now two million and six years old."

I ask again: what do we really know about dinosaurs? You can ask any real scholar in any field and he will admit that he is no authority—he hasn't mastered his field. He will frankly say that he is just beginning to learn.

May I say to you that no man is in any position to pass judgment on God. That is what God told Job way back yonder at the dawn of history.

JOB REPENTS

Now notice the effect upon Job:

Then Job answered the LORD, and said,

I know that thou canst do every thing, and that no thought can be withholden from thee [Job 42:1–2].

Is that the kind of God you have? Can He do anything?

There is the old saw about God: "Can God make a rock so big that He can't lift it?" That is like the question to Mr. Milquetoast, "Are you still beating your wife?" You see, there is no answer because you are caught whether you answer it yes or no. The question about God has no answer because God never does anything foolish. He always does that which is in the context of His character. He is always true to Himself. So you cannot tell God to do something that He cannot do. Do you know why not? Because, my friend, you are in no position to do that. God is not your errand boy. God is not going to jump through any hoop just because you hold it up.

Who is he that hideth counsel without knowledge? therefore have I uttered that I understood not; things too wonderful for me, which I knew not [Job 42:3].

Job admits he has been talking about things he doesn't know anything about. That is the way it was with our bull sessions in the college dorm. We would finish studying at night and would meet in some room and say, "What are we going to talk about?" I used to say, "Let's talk about something we don't know anything about. Then the sky's the limit. We can say anything we want to say." This is what Job has been doing. He has been talking about things he knows nothing about. He talked about things too wonderful for him, which he knew not. He has been talking without knowledge.

Hear, I beseech thee, and I will speak: I will demand of thee, and declare thou unto me.

I have heard of thee by the hearing of the ear: but now mine eye seeth thee.

**Wherefore I abhor myself, and repent in dust and ashes
[Job 42:4–6].**

Now this man Job has a new conception of God. He is not in a position
to question God in anything that He does. He is to trust Him. He is in a
new relationship.

First, Job saw himself as he really was, and he came into a new
relationship with himself. He saw himself as vile; he abhorred himself. Now he sees himself in a new relationship to God. He repents in
dust and ashes.

Here are the steps of real repentance. This is the repentance that is
in faith. First, you must see yourself as vile. Secondly, you must abhor
yourself. Perhaps you have seen birds feeding on carrion in the wilder-
ness. When you quit trusting yourself and quit trying to live on the old
dead carcass of self and you turn to the living God, that is real repentance. What a wonderful thing it is!

Job recognizes the sovereignty of God. He confesses his sin and
repents. God has accomplished His purpose in the life of Job. Job evidently realizes that the reason God has permitted him to suffer is to
bring him to repentance. He sees himself in the light of the presence of
God. "If we say that we have fellowship with him, and walk in darkness, we lie, and do not the truth: But if we walk in the light, as he is in
the light, we have fellowship one with another, and the blood of Jesus
Christ his Son cleanseth us from all sin" (1 John 1:6–7).

EPILOGUE

Finally, we find that Job also comes to a new relationship with his
friends.

> **And it was so, that after the LORD had spoken these
> words unto Job, the LORD said to Eliphaz the Temanite,
> My wrath is kindled against thee, and against thy two
> friends: for ye have not spoken of me the thing that is
> right, as my servant Job hath.**

> **Therefore take unto you now seven bullocks and seven rams, and go to my servant Job, and offer up for yourselves a burnt offering; and my servant Job shall pray for you: for him will I accept: lest I deal with you after your folly, in that ye have not spoken of me the thing which is right, like my servant Job.**

> **So Eliphaz the Temanite and Bildad the Shuhite and Zophar the Naamathite went, and did according as the LORD commanded them: the LORD also accepted Job [Job 42:7–9].**

Instead of fighting against his friends or debating them, he is now going to pray for them. He is going to offer a sacrifice for them. We are not to argue religion today or to fight among ourselves. What is it that we are to do? Paul writes, "Brethren, if a man be overtaken in a fault, ye which are spiritual, restore such an one in the spirit of meekness . . ." (Gal. 6:1). Job has a new relationship with himself, with God, and with his friends. Now God does something for Job.

> **And the LORD turned the captivity of Job, when he prayed for his friends: also the LORD gave Job twice as much as he had before [Job 42:10].**

Now, how did God give Job twice as much? He used human means.

> **Then came there unto him all his brethren, and all his sisters, and all they that had been of his acquaintance before, and did eat bread with him in his house: and they bemoaned him, and comforted him over all the evil that the LORD had brought upon him: every man also gave him a piece of money, and every one an earring of gold [Job 42:11].**

This is the way he got started. These friends staked him to a new beginning and, believe me, Job was a good business man. God gave him twice as much as he had had at the very beginning.

> So the Lord blessed the latter end of Job more than his beginning: for he had fourteen thousand sheep, and six thousand camels, and a thousand yoke of oxen, and a thousand she asses.

> He had also seven sons and three daughters [Job 42:12–13].

All of the animals were doubled. But it says here, "He had also seven sons and daughters." Someone will say, "God didn't double them." Yes, He did. You see, Job did not lose those sons and daughters who died. They were still his. He was yet to be with them. He is with them today.

We do not lose our loved ones in death. I have a little one up there. I used to tell people that I have two daughters, and they would look around and see only one. They would think there was something wrong with me. But, you see, I have one in heaven. Very frankly, I am not at all worried about my little one in heaven, I worry about the one on earth.

> And he called the name of the first, Jemima; and the name of the second, Kezia; and the name of the third, Kerenhappuch.

> And in all the land were no women found so fair as the daughters of Job: and their father gave them inheritance among their brethren [Job 42:14–15].

Now, friend, if you have quite a few daughters in your family and you are trying to think of a new name, I have a suggestion for you. Jemima would not be so good to use because there is a pancake mix sold in the United States called "Aunt Jemima." But how about Kerenhappuch? Wouldn't you like that for a name for a little girl? Or do you like Kezia?

> After this lived Job an hundred and forty years, and saw his sons, and his sons' sons, even four generations.

> So Job died, being old and full of days [Job 42:16–17].

We are told that after this Job lived 140 years. This puts him back in the age of the patriarchs. Even after all this had happened to him, he lived to see his sons and his sons' sons, even four generations. When he died, he was old and full of days.

BIBLIOGRAPHY

(Recommended for Further Study)

Archer, Gleason L. *The Book of Job*. Grand Rapids, Michigan: Baker Book House, 1982.

Blair, J. Allen. *Job: Living Patiently*. Reprint. Neptune, New Jersey: Loizeaux Brothers, 1966.

Darby, J. N. *Synopsis of the Books of the Bible*. Addison, Illinois: Bible Truth Publishers, n.d.

Ellison, H. L. *A Study of Job: From Tragedy to Triumph*. Grand Rapids, Michigan: Zondervan Publishing House, n.d.

Epp, Theodore H. *Job—A Man Tried as Gold*. Lincoln, Nebraska: Back to the Bible Broadcast, n.d.

Gaebelein, Arno C. *The Annotated Bible*. 1917. Reprint. Neptune, New Jersey: Loizeaux Brothers, 1971.

Garland, D. David. *Job—A Study Guide Commentary*. Grand Rapids, Michigan: Zondervan Publishing House, 1971.

Gray, James M. *Synthetic Bible Studies*. Westwood, New Jersey: Fleming H. Revell Co., 1906.

Jensen, Irving L. *Job—A Self Study Guide*. Chicago, Illinois: Moody Press, 1975.

Mackintosh, C. H. *Miscellaneous Writings*. Reprint. Neptune, New Jersey: Loizeaux Brothers, 1976.

Ridout, Samuel. *The Book of Job*. Neptune, New Jersey: Loizeaux Brothers, 1919. (Very fine)

Sauer, Erich. *The Dawn of World Redemption*. Grand Rapids, Michigan: Wm. B. Eerdmans Publishing Co., 1951. (An excellent Old Testament survey)

Scroggie, W. Graham. *The Unfolding Drama of Redemption*. Grand Rapids, Michigan: Zondervan Publishing House, 1970. (An excellent survey and outline of the Old Testament)

Unger, Merrill F. *Unger's Bible Handbook*. Chicago, Illinois: Moody Press, 1966. (A concise commentary on the entire Bible)

Unger, Merrill F. *Unger's Commentary on the Old Testament*. Vol. 1. Chicago, Illinois: Moody Press, 1981. (A fine summary of each paragraph—Highly recommended)

Zuck, Roy B. *Job*. Chicago, Illinois: Moody Press, 1978. (A fine summary—see the *Everyman's Bible Commentary* series)